MW01196977

The Official LORE OLYMPUS Cookbook

Foreword by
RACHEL SMYTHE

Recipes by
DIANA MOUTSOPOULOS

Written by
GENN McMENEMY

Photography by
EVA KOLENKO

The Official LORE OLYMPUS Cookbook

RANDOM HOUSE WORLDS

NEW YORK

For my mom and dad
— GENN McMENEMY

For A1 and A2, my best recipe testers
— DIANA MOUTSOPOULOS

To Emy Koller
—RACHEL SMYTHE

CONTENTS

Fall

Fall Harvest Festival Feast

Winter

Winter Wedding Feast

FOREWORD

Food is important to storytelling, and Lore Olympus is no exception.

Artemis can't cook. It might be a bit strange to open a cookbook talking about a character who is no good at it, but the thing about food is that it can tell us so much about a person, a place, their culture, and the world they live in. What people cook and why people cook bring a story to life.

When Artemis attempts to bake Persephone a cake as an apology, it's clear that things have not gone well in the kitchen. She didn't wait for the cake to cool, so the frosting slid off. The lopsided shape seems to suggest it might not be cooked all the way through. The cake is bad. That said, it's also good!

Artemis's cake is certainly no culinary masterpiece, but it's an act of vulnerability. We now know Artemis is willing to set

her ego aside and do something she is not familiar with, just so she can put her new roommate at ease.

Artemis and her cake appear in stark contrast to the behavior of her twin brother, Apollo, who is so confident in his abilities that he not only invites himself over to make breakfast, but he also brings a whole crepe station.

Food, and how people treat it, helps tell the story.

When Persephone offhandedly comments that she's altered Hestia's baklava recipe, it's not just about the taste; it's about the act of defiance. This grants us a small insight into Persephone's state of mind and foreshadows what's to come in her journey.

When Hades goes to the market to buy dinner supplies for his "not date" with Minthe, this shows he opts to do things himself, even though he has the means to send someone else if he wants to. He also thinks the evening is

significant enough to put the effort in, which makes it all the more upsetting when Minthe doesn't show. I think the emotional impact hits harder because Hades made the meal. If he'd been stood up at a restaurant, it wouldn't have been as hurtful.

As a writer, I feel that food helps us as readers gather information about characters in a way that feels natural. We all eat, after all. The inclusion of any food is small, but it goes a long way. Much like the use of fashion or colors, the language of food is an integral part of the storytelling of *Lore Olympus*.

For that reason, I am so delighted to share with you this official cookbook to further enrich your participation in the world of *Lore Olympus*.

May your cakes be more successful than Artemis's, but made with as much love.

—RACHEL SMYTHE

INTRODUCTION

Welcome one and all to The Official Lore Olympus Cookbook

Whether you're a new fan or a longtime reader—or maybe even a god disguised as a human, looking for some new fare to dazzle your fellow Olympians—there is something for everyone in this delectable tome.

The world of *Lore Olympus* is a sumptuous one, filled with color, drama, mystery, friendship, love, and food. It is a world that you can easily escape into again and again, a love story for the ages that follows Persephone and Hades as they grow and change and fall deeper in love. The tale's origins go all the way back to ancient times and have been replayed through the centuries in fiction. But in *Lore Olympus,* we get a new take on a classic.

Persephone, the beautiful young maiden with a terrible secret. Hades, the lonely and jaded god who falls instantly in love the moment he lays eyes on her. She is the goddess of spring who belongs to the sunlight and fields. He is the god of the Underworld, who makes his home below the ground, far away from the warmth of the mortal realm.

They are an unlikely couple—and they somehow find a way to bring out the best in each other.

Rachel Smythe's reimagining is a delightful melding of the ancient myths and the modern world. It constantly reinvents and plays with the mythology so that the stories become fresh and relevant for today's readers.

The mythology takes on its own life, growing and adapting alongside its protagonists, allowing readers to find themselves in the characters of Hades, Persephone, Hera, Eros, and so many more. It invites us into a world of gods, gossip, snark, and friendship—and whether you are following Hades's day in the Underworld or wandering the fields of the mortal realm with Demeter, it is easy to feel like you are a part of the pantheon. Hoping that Hades will find the courage to let himself love and be loved, or that Demeter will finally be able to let her daughter bloom and grow like the fields around her.

But more than being immersive, the story asks us to evolve alongside it, to practice empathy and compassion—even, in the end, for Minthe! It gives a voice and representation to so many people who have been left out or unheard for so long. It begs the reader not to look away, even from the difficult moments; to bear witness. It is a story filled with joy, growth, and finding oneself, even in the darkest of times and places. *Lore Olympus* teaches readers that it's OK to be a work in progress. And it's OK not to have all the answers and to ask for help. To try new things in order to grow as a person (or as a god, as the case may be).

It is the type of feeling that leads directly to the heart of good cooking. Cooking is something that, as a species, we've been doing since prehistoric times—since Prometheus angered Zeus and brought humans fire—and it is an expression of love, a necessity for survival, and what brings us together as families and communities.

This cookbook will teach you how to make some of the most famous meals in *Lore Olympus* (Persephone's Baklava, Hera's Moussaka, Eros's Apology Donuts), but it won't contain every food item featured in the comics. Instead, this book will show you how to cook some of the best-loved Greek dishes—like souvlaki, tzatziki, shrimp saganaki, and more—in new and exciting ways, and using seasonally appropriate ingredients.

Organized by season, which is the perfect way to eat, each chapter offers a recipe for any time of the day, whether you are hankering for breakfast, lunch, dinner, or a bright pink cocktail. And just in case you want to share food with your fellow *Lore Olympus* lovers, there is a feast at the end of each section, serving as inspiration for a themed party to close out the season.

Like *Lore Olympus*, this cookbook is a new take on an old classic, with recipes that breathe fresh life into traditional Greek cuisine. It is approachable for cooks of all skill levels, and gives detailed step-by-step instructions to make sure that no dish is off-limits, allowing you to create feasts fit for the Olympians. And us lucky mortals.

Spring

A *Celebration* OF *Persephone*

Spring is Persephone's season: filled with growth, transformation, and new life. On the surface, spring seems light and joyous, the moment when the world wakes up from its winter slumber and everything seems to burst into bloom all at once in a riot of color. When we throw open our shutters to breathe in the fresh air, and also release the old things that we have been holding on to.

At least, that is the story we've been telling ourselves for millennia.

But spring has a darker undertone. It is also filled with violent storms and snowmelts that rush down from the mountains, causing rivers to flood and

wild seas to wake. The light air of spring always carries with it the undertone of death—and perhaps that is why Persephone is a goddess of both.

Spring, like Persephone, comes with a little bit of wrath. It is this darkness—*this feeling,* as Persephone calls it in the comic— that allows for change, rebirth, and growth. In order for some things to flourish, others must die. Spring is when the rains bring life to some crops and drown others; it is when new creatures are born and when predators awaken from hibernation.

Hades only gets to experience Persephone's version of spring one time in *Lore Olympus,* when he visits the mortal world to check on his unusually active volcanoes. He wonders if perhaps Demeter is having a midlife crisis when he arrives, because the verdant landscape is chaotic and haphazard, but also beautiful and so full of life. These contradictions are what made Persephone one of the most formidable gods in the Greek pantheon. Mortals feared her as much as they feared Hades—they called her the Dread Queen.

While in the Underworld, she had as much power and respect as her husband. In the mortal realm, she was revered for the very traits that frustrate Persephone so much in *Lore Olympus.* She was both the beautiful maiden, Kore, and the terrifying "Bringer of Death," Persephone. And her story was always tied closely to her relationships with both her mother and her husband.

Worship of Persephone traditionally revolved around the seasons. Cyclically, she was celebrated during the Eleusinian Mysteries, which were rites that took place in the town of Eleusis, to the north of Athens. Every autumn and spring, worshipers would

reenact the story of Persephone's journey to the Underworld. Starting in Athens in the ancient cemetery of Kerameikos, crowds would leave the land of the dead and travel north to the temple of Eleusis, where they would enter the sacred cave. Inside this cave, Persephone would either descend into the Underworld by a series of pulleys and platforms or ascend from the depths back into the mortal realm.

The mystery cult of Persephone and Demeter didn't just follow the seasons of the natural world; it also replicated the seasons of a woman's life. Women were initiated into the cult when they reached marriageable age, and

while the rites still remain a secret, scholars have suggested that they were rooted in the transition from girlhood to wifehood and then to eventual motherhood.

But this wasn't where the worship of Persephone stopped. Persephone, Demeter, and Hecate eventually became three sides of more modern religions—the Maiden, Mother, and Crone that we see in Wiccan and other pagan beliefs. Together, they represent the different sides of the divine feminine, the triple aspects of the goddess.

In the universe of *Lore Olympus*, Persephone begins her story as a girl looking to carve out a place for herself in the world. She is terrified of her own inner darkness, which, according to Eris and Ares, makes her "interesting." She is afraid of herself and who she could become. So she hides that fear with bright colors and by making herself small and unassuming. As she grows throughout the series, she embraces her darkness and transforms into a queen and leader. One who is kind and caring and giving, and also just a little bit terrifying.

A true goddess of spring.

The recipes included in this section celebrate the contradictions and reflect the seasonal ingredients, delicious flavors, and sweet scents of spring. Try a refreshing strawberry lemonade, or a zesty and herbal frittata. Indulge in the rich and complex flavors of a stew, or a tangy spanakopita pasta bake. Flex your baking muscles with gloriously fruity cinnamon rolls, or put a subtle twist on a classic with lemon loukoumi.

Whether you're preparing a feast for friends who have shaken off their winter hibernation or want the ultimate girl dinner during a solo night in, these meals will help you embrace your own inner kitchen goddess.

Fennel Frond Frittata

Serves — 2 to 4   *Prep time* — 10 minutes   *Cook time* — 15 minutes

Brunch is the greatest meal of the day. It combines all the best things: breakfast and lunch, prosecco and Bloody Marys, savory and sweet dishes. It is a celebration of all the best things in life, and is the favorite meal of Dionysus—god of wine and parties, and also the foster child of Persephone and Hades. And the fennel plant just so happens to be sacred to him!

The green leaves of the fennel bulb are an underutilized part of the plant, but they are so versatile in cooking, adding just a hint of licorice flavor to any dish. These flavorful frittatas wield this secret weapon to perfection, and are easy to scale up or down to make a meal for one or a feast for your brunch crew.

1 tablespoon extra-virgin olive oil

3 green onions, chopped

½ cup (15 g) chopped fennel fronds

6 large eggs, beaten

salt and pepper, to taste

4 oz (110 g) sheep's-milk feta cheese, crumbled

1. Preheat the oven's broiler.

2. On the stovetop, heat the olive oil in an ovenproof 8-inch (20 cm) frying pan over medium heat. Add the green onion and cook until softened, 3 to 4 minutes. Add the fennel fronds and cook, stirring, for 1 minute.

3. Pour in the eggs and season with salt and pepper. Once the bottom is set, sprinkle the top of the frittata with the feta.

4. Broil until the center is set and the top is browned, 5 to 8 minutes. Serve.

Dionysus
Worship of Dionysus involved the fennel plant. Fennel stalks were often used to create a thyrsus—a spear-like staff that was wrapped with vines and topped with a pine cone and ribbons. Thyrsi were carried by priestesses and priests of Dionysus and were involved in the theatrical rituals dedicated to the god.

Demeter's Braised Spring Vegetable Stew

Serves — 4   *Prep time* — 15 minutes   *Cook time* — 30 minutes

In the comic, spring has always been predictable—until Persephone returns from the Underworld as queen. Something has gone wrong with her powers and, in turn, with the season. Her return to the mortal realm brings snow and cold to the world. Hebe gets caught up in the snowstorm and is taken to Demeter, who warms her up with a heart-to-heart and a steaming bowl of vegetable stew.

Our take on Demeter's hearty stew is made with fresh, in-season vegetables like fennel, peas, onions, and carrots—and it's the perfect meal to carry you through the transitional days of early spring and into the warmth of the new season.

⅓ cup (75 ml) extra-virgin
  olive oil
6 green onions, chopped
2 large carrots, cut into 2-inch
  (5 cm) chunks
1 fennel bulb, sliced
2 cups (225 g) shelled English peas
  or frozen peas
8 to 10 baby yellow potatoes,
  peeled
1 cup (30 g) chopped fennel fronds
  or dill
salt and pepper, to taste
juice of 1 small lemon
1 teaspoon cornstarch

1. Heat the olive oil in a large saucepan or Dutch oven over medium heat. Add the green onion and cook until just softened, 2 to 3 minutes. Add the carrots, fennel, and peas. Cook, stirring, 1 to 2 minutes. Add the potatoes, fennel fronds, and salt and pepper. (See note.)

2. Pour in water to just barely cover the vegetables. Bring to a boil, then reduce the heat and simmer gently, partially covered, until all the vegetables are tender, 15 to 20 minutes. Remove the lid toward the end of cooking to help reduce the cooking liquid in the pan.

3. Just before serving, mix the lemon juice with the cornstarch to make a slurry. Stir into the pan and cook a few minutes more over medium heat until the sauce is thickened.

COOK'S NOTE: *You can also add artichoke hearts to this stew, if desired, which is a common addition in a similar dish called Artichokes à la Polita (artichokes of the city). To make Artichokes à la Polita, omit the fennel bulb and add 6 to 8 whole cleaned artichoke hearts at the same time as the carrots and peas in step 1.*

A Year Without Spring?

In human history there have been several years without spring or summer. These happened after large volcanic eruptions that ejected huge quantities of ash and other material into the atmosphere, creating a barrier to the sun's warmth and light. Now we understand that this is called a volcanic winter, and that a volcano on the other side of the world can actually impact the weather. But in the ancient world, this wasn't as well understood. So there were many different festivals held yearly to ensure that the sun would return and that the seasons would change. One possible time the ancient Greeks might have experienced this lack of a spring and summer was at the start of the Bronze Age collapse/decline, which may have been caused by the enormous volcanic eruption at Thera circa 1600 B.C.E.

Saucy Baked Giant Beans

Serves — 6   *Prep time* — 10 minutes   *Cook time* — 1¾ hours   *Extra time* — 8 hours, soaking

Beans are essential in the Greek diet—and, in fact, beans were so important to the ancient diet that there was once a god of beans. Not much is known about Kyamites, except that he was a key figure in the Eleusinian Mysteries cult, and was worshiped alongside Demeter and Persephone. He is referenced in only two places: in a small roadside sanctuary dedicated to him that stood between Athens and Eleusis, and in a travelogue.

Giant beans (or giant butter beans) are the star of this dish, covered in a garlicky tomato sauce and then baked. These are popular as a meze or side dish, or you can add some sausage, crusty bread, feta, or salad and make a meal out of them. And unlike the enigmatic god Kyamites, it's no mystery as to why this dish is so popular in Greece—and why it will be a hit in your own kitchen, too!

FOR THE BEANS

1 lb (450 g) dried giant beans or
    butter beans (see tip)
8 cups (2 L) filtered water
½ teaspoon salt

FOR THE BAKE

1 jarred roasted red pepper, finely
    chopped
1 small carrot, diced
1⅔ cups (400 g) strained tomatoes
    (passata) or crushed tomatoes
½ cup (120 ml) extra-virgin
    olive oil
3 tablespoons chopped fresh
    parsley
3 cloves garlic, crushed into a paste
2 bay leaves
1 teaspoon salt, or to taste
pepper, to taste
11 oz (300 g) sausage, such as
    Portuguese, Italian, or Greek
    loukaniko, cut into 1-inch
    (2.5 cm) slices (optional)

1. Prepare the beans: Place the dried beans in a bowl and cover with plenty of water. Soak for 8 hours or overnight. Drain well and rinse.

2. Place the beans, filtered water, and salt in a large pot over medium-high heat. Cover and bring to a boil, then reduce the heat to medium and cook, covered, until the beans are just tender, 50 to 60 minutes. Remove from the heat. At this point, you can let the beans cool and refrigerate them to bake the next day, if desired.

3. Meanwhile, preheat the oven to 400 degrees F (200 degrees C). Drain the beans, reserving the cooking liquid.

4. Make the bake: Place the drained beans in a 9-by-13-inch (20 by 30 cm) baking dish. Add 1 cup (240 ml) of the reserved bean cooking liquid along with the roasted red pepper, carrot, tomatoes, olive oil, parsley, garlic, bay leaves, salt, and pepper. Stir gently to evenly distribute the ingredients. Lay the sliced sausage, if using, in an even layer over the top.

5. Bake in the preheated oven until the sausage is browned and the sauce has thickened and is bubbling, 45 to 50 minutes. Let cool slightly before serving.

TIP: *For a shortcut, use canned beans instead of dried. Choose canned beans with no added salt; you will need three 15-oz cans. Follow the recipe from step 3. If you can't find canned butter beans, you can try almost any white bean or borlotti beans.*

Spanakopita Pasta Bake

Serves — 4   *Prep time* — 15 minutes   *Cook time* — 30 minutes

Spanakopita is a traditional Greek dish. The flaky phyllo pastry, the creamy feta, and the earthy spinach make for a delicious dish that can be anything from an appetizer to a main course. You can find it everywhere across Greece, from restaurants in Athens to tavernas in the mountains of Arcadia to out-of-the-way seaside island cafes across the Aegean.

And, much like in *Lore Olympus*, everyone has their own version of the classic dish. This take is a crowd-pleaser, perfect for batch cooking to savor all week long—especially if you are on a budget, like Persephone—or for sharing with your friends and family. It's the ideal meal to have in your fridge, too, in the event of a surprise visit from Eros, Hermes, or flower nymphs with poor boundaries who show up with or without an invitation.

---

8 oz (225 g) short pasta in the shape of your choice, such as shells or penne

3 tablespoons extra-virgin olive oil, divided

4 green onions, chopped

10 oz (280 g) fresh baby spinach leaves (see tip and note)

1 pinch salt

¾ cup (180 ml) heavy cream

¼ cup (60 ml) whole milk

4 oz (110 g) cream cheese

7 oz (200 g) sheep's-milk feta cheese, crumbled

1 cup (30 g) chopped fresh dill

pepper, to taste

½ cup (40 g) breadcrumbs, preferably panko

Butter or cooking spray, for greasing the baking dish

1. Bring a large pot of salted water to a boil. Add the pasta and cook according to the package directions. Drain well, but do not rinse. Return to the pot and set aside.

2. Preheat the oven to 400 degrees F (200 degrees C). Grease a 9-inch (23 cm) square baking dish.

3. Heat 2 tablespoons olive oil in a large frying or sauté pan over medium heat. Add the green onions and cook gently until they begin to soften, about 3 minutes. Increase the heat to medium high and add the spinach and salt; cook, stirring, until the spinach is wilted and any excess liquid has evaporated, 5 to 8 minutes.

TIP: *It'll seem like a lot of spinach at first, more than can fit in your pan! Add the spinach in batches, cooking the first batch until wilted before adding more.*

4. Add the cream and milk to the spinach mixture and bring to a gentle simmer. Stir in the cream cheese and break apart with a spoon, cooking just until melted.

Hades and Animals

Sheep, cattle, and black rams are all animals associated with Hades. Although Hades was often feared by mortals and worship of him was done in secret, historians believe black rams were his preferred sacrifice.

Another animal associated with the god of the Underworld? Dogs. Hades's love of dogs—in particular his three-headed pup, Cerberus—is widely portrayed in ancient artwork. Cerberus was not known for herding sheep, however; instead, he shepherded the souls of the dead in the Underworld.

5. Remove the pan from the heat and stir in the crumbled feta, chopped dill, and pepper. Add the cooked pasta and stir until well combined, then spoon into the prepared baking dish. Cover with the breadcrumbs and then drizzle with the remaining olive oil.

6. Bake in the preheated oven until the topping is golden and the sauce is bubbling around the edges, 15 to 20 minutes. Let cool slightly before serving.

COOK'S NOTE: *Spring's fresh spinach shines here, but you could easily enjoy this any time of year with frozen spinach.*

Pan-Fried Lamb Chops Lemonato

Serves — 4   *Prep time* — 5 minutes   *Cook time* — 10 minutes   *Extra time* — 30 minutes, marinating

Lambs and sheep appear throughout Greek mythology. Rams in particular were said to be a symbol of protection. Famously, Jason goes on the quest to steal the golden ram's fleece and bring it back to his homeland. And Psyche is tasked with gathering the golden wool of vicious, poisonous sheep during her quest to reunite with Eros.

Unlike Psyche and Jason, you won't have to go to the ends of the earth and face dragons and man-eating sheep to enjoy this recipe. All you have to do is pick a side dish like a village salad or lemon roasted potatoes, and then remember to marinate the lamb for 30 minutes.

5 tablespoons extra-virgin olive oil, divided

2½ teaspoons salt

pepper, to taste

2 lb lamb rib chops (8 to 10 chops)

¾ cup (180 ml) freshly squeezed lemon juice

1 teaspoon dried Greek oregano, plus extra for garnish

1. In a resealable plastic bag or container, combine 3 tablespoons olive oil and the salt and pepper. Add the lamb chops and coat all sides in the olive oil mixture. Set aside and let rest at room temperature for 30 minutes.

2. In a large frying pan, heat 2 tablespoons olive oil over medium-high heat. When the oil is hot and shimmering, add half of the lamb chops. Sear for 2 minutes on one side until browned, then flip and sear an additional 2 minutes. Remove the chops from the pan to a plate and let them rest while you repeat the process with the remaining lamb chops.

3. Once all the lamb chops have been seared and browned, add the lamb chops from the plate back to the pan. Pour in the lemon juice and sprinkle with the oregano. Simmer for 1 to 2 minutes, letting the juices reduce slightly and coat the lamb chops.

4. Remove from the heat and serve immediately with a little oregano sprinkled over the top.

Lemony Sautéed Greens and Chickpeas

Serves — 4   *Prep time* — 10 minutes   *Cook time* — 15 minutes

Helios, the Titan of the sun and the surly font of all Olympian gossip, gets only a very short rest each day as he wanders around the earth in his role as both sun and sun god. Barely enough time to cook and eat a meal! Luckily, with this simple and fast vegan dish, you get to enjoy the best things—lemons, spinach, chickpeas, and garlic—in under 15 minutes. That leaves you plenty of time to enjoy this riff on spanakorizo, a traditional Greek spinach and rice dish, before you have to get back to your day shift.

1 small onion

2 large garlic cloves, halved

5 tablespoons extra-virgin olive oil, divided

1 tablespoon tomato paste

1 bunch Swiss chard, roughly chopped

2 pinches salt, plus more to taste

10 oz (280 g) fresh baby spinach leaves

1 can (15 oz / 425 g) no-salt-added chickpeas, drained and liquid reserved

pepper, to taste

1 lemon, quartered

1. Grate the onion on the large holes of a box grater. Place the onion, garlic, and 4 tablespoons olive oil in a large shallow sauté pan over medium heat. Sauté until the onion has softened, 5 to 8 minutes.

2. Stir the tomato paste into the onion mixture and cook until the paste has darkened in color, 1 to 2 minutes.

3. Add the Swiss chard and a generous pinch of salt. Cook until wilted and reduced to about half its volume, then add the spinach and another pinch of salt. Cook, stirring occasionally, until the spinach is almost all wilted, 2 to 3 minutes.

4. Add the drained chickpeas and ¼ cup (60 ml) of the reserved bean liquid. Partially cover and cook gently until all the greens are wilted and there's little excess liquid in the pan, 3 to 5 minutes. Season with salt and pepper, stir well, and remove from the heat. Serve with the lemon wedges and drizzle with 1 tablespoon olive oil.

COOK'S NOTE: *This makes a bright side dish for four or a satisfying vegan main for two.*

[WHAT IS SNARKY CHAT?]

SNARKY CHAT IS AN
ONGOING FATESBOOK
MESSAGE CONVERSATION...

WHICH IS SHARED BY
THANATOS, MINTHE,
AND THETIS.

SNARKY CHAT WAS ESTABLISHED
APPROXIMATELY 8 MONTHS AGO FOR
THE EXPRESS PURPOSE OF TALKING
SHIT ABOUT OTHER PEOPLE.

Arugula Salad with Grape Molasses Vinaigrette

Serves — 4   *Prep time* — 10 minutes   *Cook time* — 5 minutes

Minthe and Thetis are the typical mean girls of *Lore Olympus*. Together with Thanatos, they form a "Snarky Chat" to secretly badmouth people, pick at the flaws of others, and even needle themselves into periods of insecurity. For a long time, Minthe thinks that what she has with Thetis is a friendship. She doesn't understand that friendships should not hurt. They should be supportive, with friends trying to help each other do better and be happier.

It's not until Minthe is among the nymphs of the mortal realm that she learns what friendship should be: sweet with an occasional peppery bite, plus some nuts who are a little cheesy and who sometimes indulge in a splash of red wine (and gossip). It should be just like this recipe, filled with delicious ingredients to support your body and soul.

FOR THE SALAD

¼ cup (50 g) golden raisins or sultanas
2½ tablespoons lemon juice
⅓ cup (30 g) flaked almonds
5 cups (140 g) arugula
4 oz (110 g) Graviera or Manchego cheese

FOR THE VINAIGRETTE

¼ cup (60 ml) extra-virgin olive oil
2½ tablespoons (40 ml) red wine vinegar
1 tablespoon (15 ml) Dijon mustard
1 tablespoon (15 ml) grape molasses or petimezi (see note)
salt and pepper, to taste

1. Make the salad: Place the raisins and lemon juice in a small bowl and set aside.

2. Place the flaked almonds in a small frying pan over medium heat. Gently toast until evenly golden brown, stirring occasionally, about 5 minutes. Remove from the heat and set aside.

3. Make the vinaigrette: Combine the olive oil, vinegar, mustard, and grape molasses in a clean jam or canning jar. Close the lid and shake well, until homogeneous and emulsified. Season with salt and pepper, then close the lid and shake once more.

4. Assemble the salad: Lay the arugula in a large serving platter or salad bowl. Use a vegetable peeler to shave the cheese over the top. Sprinkle with the almonds. Drain the raisins and scatter on top. Pour the vinaigrette over the salad and serve.

COOK'S NOTE: *Grape molasses can be found in Middle Eastern stores and is very similar to a Greek version called petimezi. If you have trouble finding it, you can substitute date syrup or honey.*

Lemon Roasted Potatoes

Serves — 4   *Prep time* — 15 minutes   *Cook time* — 1¼ to 1½ hours

Nothing invokes the Mediterranean quite like lemons. The bright color, inviting scent, and zesty flavor they add bring joy to every dish. Couple lemons and delicious crispy roasted potatoes and you have a recipe that's love at first bite.

Potatoes and lemons are not native to Greece, but since their arrival, they have shaken up the country's cuisine. Much like Eris, the goddess of discord, these two staples brought with them massive disruption. And while Eris is feared by all the gods because she sows chaos wherever she goes, without her power there would be no change. Everything would stay stagnant. And though change can be a thing to fear, sometimes change is . . . lemons and potatoes. Two ingredients that transformed the Greek diet in the most wonderful way.

6 large yellow or Yukon Gold potatoes, peeled and cut into thin wedges (2¼ lb / 1 kg)
¾ cup (180 ml) water, plus more if needed
½ cup (120 ml) lemon juice
⅓ cup (75 ml) extra-virgin olive oil
1 tablespoon Dijon or yellow mustard
1 teaspoon dried Greek oregano
salt and pepper, to taste

1. Preheat the oven to 350 degrees F (180 degrees C).

2. Place the potato wedges in a 9-by-13-inch (23 by 33 cm) baking dish. Mix the water, lemon juice, olive oil, mustard, oregano, and salt and pepper together. Add to the potatoes, stir to coat, and arrange in a single layer.

3. Bake in the preheated oven, carefully turning over halfway through, until the potatoes are tender and nearly all the excess liquid has evaporated, 1¼ to 1½ hours. Check occasionally to ensure the potatoes aren't drying out too much; add up to ½ cup (120 ml) water at the halfway point if needed. Resist stirring too often, so as not to break up the starch and affect the consistency of the potatoes. Broil briefly at the end of roasting if a little char is desired on the top of the potatoes. Serve.

Hecate's Homebrew Aegean Flip

Serves — 1   *Prep time* — 10 minutes

In *Lore Olympus,* Hecate is a fashion maven, a threefold goddess, and one of the few beings Zeus is actually scared of. She is always there to fix the crowns of other queens (and the King of the Underworld), acting as wise counsel, a compassionate friend, and the voice of reason when Hades (or Thanatos) needs a reminder of who's really in charge: Hecate. Not to mention she's very knowledgeable about poison and potions.

It's witchcraft how this cocktail changes color. Or is it? This showstopping concoction is something Hecate, the Titaness and goddess of witchcraft, would love. Hecate's blue brew is a fun take on a traditional flip—although it uses only egg whites, not whole eggs. By adding butterfly pea flower powder, this decadent drink changes color right before your eyes. Glow up your hosting game and serve a truly magical cocktail.

2 fl oz (60 ml) gin of your choice
  (see tip and note)
¾ fl oz (20 ml) simple syrup
  (page 123)
¼ fl oz (7 ml) orange blossom
  water
¼ teaspoon butterfly pea flower
  powder
1 egg white

1. Combine the gin, simple syrup, orange blossom water, and butterfly pea flower powder in a cocktail shaker full of ice. Shake vigorously until the outside of the shaker is frosty, 20 to 30 seconds. Strain into a coupe glass and discard the ice.

2. Return the gin mixture to the cocktail shaker along with the egg white. Cover and shake vigorously for 1 minute, until foamy. Pour back into the glass and serve.

TIP: *The mocktail version of this drink is purple, so they're easy to tell apart! Combine ⅓ cup (75 ml) lemonade, ⅓ fl oz (10 ml) simple syrup, ¼ fl oz (7 ml) orange blossom water, and ¼ teaspoon butterfly pea flower powder in a cocktail shaker full of ice. Shake as above, then strain into a spritz glass. Top with sparkling water and garnish with a slice of lemon.*

COOK'S NOTE: *The choice of gin can affect the flavor greatly; this recipe was created with a floral variety, but feel free to use your favorite!*

Mushroom Galettes

Serves — 6   *Prep time* — 45 minutes   *Cook time* — 30 minutes

These mushroom galettes are inspired by manitaropita, Greek mushroom pie. They are small, cheesy veggie pies made with a yogurt and olive oil dough called kourou pastry. The contradiction in tastes and flavors creates a savory explosion for the taste buds.

The ancient Greeks used mushrooms in food, medicine, and rituals. Researchers think that mushrooms might have been consumed in the Eleusinian Mysteries as part of a religious ritual that simulated life, death, and rebirth.

In *Lore Olympus*, mushrooms are a big part of Persephone's vegetarian diet. When she invites Demeter to dinner, she makes a mushroom pasta bake. This reflects the ancient Greek views of mushrooms: Mushrooms could mean death and a connection to the Underworld, or they could mean rebirth and enlightenment—which is what Persephone is trying to find in her relationship with her mother.

FOR THE MUSHROOM FILLING

¼ cup (60 ml) extra-virgin olive oil
1 large onion, thinly sliced into rounds (about 1 lb / 450 g)
½ teaspoon salt, divided, plus more to taste
24 oz (680 g) baby bella mushrooms, roughly chopped
2 cups (225 g) grated cheese, such as Kasseri or Manchego
1 jarred roasted red pepper, finely chopped
½ cup (7 g) fresh mint leaves, chopped
pepper, to taste
1 egg, beaten
sesame seeds, for garnish

1. Preheat the oven to 350 degrees F (180 degrees C). Line a baking sheet with parchment paper.

2. Make the mushroom filling: Heat the olive oil in a large frying pan over medium heat. Add the onion and ¼ teaspoon salt, cover with a lid, and cook until the onion has softened, about 10 minutes, stirring occasionally.

3. Meanwhile, make the pastry: In a large mixing bowl, stir together the yogurt and olive oil until well combined. Mix the flour, baking powder, and salt in a small bowl, then add to the yogurt mixture. Stir together until combined, then lightly knead into a large ball. Set aside.

4. Add the mushrooms to the onion mixture along with ¼ teaspoon salt, and increase the heat to medium high. Cook, stirring occasionally, until the mushrooms have reduced and all the excess liquid has evaporated, 10 to 15 minutes. Remove from the heat and stir in the cheese, red pepper, mint, and pepper. Taste and add more salt, if desired. Let cool slightly before serving.

FOR THE KOUROU PASTRY

1 cup (200 g) plain Greek yogurt
    (2 to 5%)
1 cup (240 ml) extra-virgin
    olive oil
3 cups (375 g) all-purpose flour
1½ tablespoons baking powder
½ teaspoon salt

5. Divide the ball of dough in half, then roll each half into a small log and cut into thirds so that you have six pieces of pastry about the same size.

6. Roll a piece of dough to a thickness of about ⅛ inch (3 mm), creating a circle about 7 inches (18 cm) in diameter. Add approximately a sixth of the mushroom filling to the center, leaving about ½ inch (1.25 cm) around the edge. Fold the edges over to partially cover the filling. Brush all over with the beaten egg, sprinkle with sesame seeds, and place on the prepared baking sheet. Repeat with the remaining dough and filling.

7. Bake in the preheated oven until the pastry is golden brown and the filling is set, 25 to 30 minutes. Remove and let cool slightly before serving warm or at room temperature.

YOU ARE
CORDIALLY
INVITED

Spring TEA PARTY *Feast*

Aphrodite's
Rose Petal
Sugar Cookies
pg 48

Eros's Apology
Donuts
pg 58

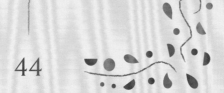

44

Strawberry
Rose Lemonade
pg 60

The Sweet
Revenge Pink
Cinnamon Rolls
pg 56

Loukoumi
pg 52

Spring is the glorious return to nature and the outdoors. It is the season when the long-dormant trees and plants burst back into life in riotous bloom. It is a time for waking up from our own winter slumbers. And in *Lore Olympus* fashion, we've put together a Spring Tea Party Feast, inspired by Persephone's many tea (and sympathy) parties with Hera. Although, in true Hera fashion, this party is less about tea and more about . . . spiked lemonade.

Afternoon tea is often thought of as a comforting catch-up with friends, but throughout the ages, it has also been a place for gathering to gossip. For millennia, people have sized up their enemies over a beverage—and Hera is no exception. Her gatherings are reconnaissance and fact-finding missions, where she collects information to lay the groundwork for her plans. Whether it's searching for a suitable husband for Persephone or plotting to overthrow Kronos, battle strategizing is better over tea and cake. And that is why Hera is our queen!

Brimming with aromatic confections and decadent cakes, this tea party is one you'll want to re-create often to enjoy on a rainy spring day indoors with your friends or outside on a picnic while you gossip about your foes.

Aphrodite's Rose Petal Sugar Cookies

Yield — 18 cookies   *Prep time* — 15 minutes   *Cook time* — 8 minutes   *Extra time* — 2 hours, chilling

Roses are a herald of spring. The delicate flowers are cultivated in gardens and bloom in the wild across Greece—and pairing fragrant roses with chewy, buttery sugar cookies is a delightful way to welcome the season.

Roses are a romantic symbol and even today are tied to love and seduction. Their heady scent is intoxicating, and the ancient Greeks used the flowers in everything—cooking, bathing, medicine, and perfume. So it's unsurprising that roses have been sacred to Aphrodite, the goddess of love, beauty, and seduction, since ancient times.

According to myth, the flowers were once only white, but Aphrodite's blood fell upon a rosebush when she was trying to warn her lover Adonis about a plot to murder him. Her blood turned the roses from white to crimson, and the flowers became forever associated with the goddess. Roses were placed on her altars in worship of her.

FOR THE COOKIES

½ cup (100 g) granulated sugar

⅓ cup (75 ml) extra-virgin olive oil

1 egg

½ teaspoon rose water

1 cup all-purpose flour

2 tablespoons crushed dried rose petals (see note)

1 teaspoon baking powder

1 pinch salt

FOR THE ICING

½ cup (60 g) powdered sugar

1 to 2 teaspoons rose water, as needed

Pink food coloring (optional)

1. Make the cookies: Beat the granulated sugar, olive oil, egg, and rose water in a bowl until smooth and pale in color. Add the flour, rose petals, baking powder, and salt and mix until just combined. Chill the dough in the refrigerator for 2 hours or overnight.

TIP: *Chilling the dough prevents the cookies from spreading and creates crackled tops.*

2. Preheat the oven to 375 degrees F (190 degrees C). Line a baking sheet with parchment paper.

3. Use a teaspoon to drop spoonfuls of the chilled dough onto the prepared baking sheet, leaving about 2 inches (5 cm) of space between the cookies. Refrigerate any leftover dough to bake in batches.

4. Bake in the preheated oven until just golden around the edges, 7 to 8 minutes. Allow to cool for 2 minutes on the baking sheet before transferring to a cooling rack.

5. Once the cookies are cool, make the icing: Mix together the powdered sugar and rose water. Start with 1 teaspoon rose water and add more until a drizzling consistency is reached. Add a small drop of pink food coloring to the icing mixture, if desired, for a more vibrant color.

6. Drizzle the cooled cookies with the icing. Store the cookies in an airtight container, with waxed paper between the layers.

Loukoumi

Yield — 64 pieces *Prep time* — 30 minutes *Cook time* — 1½ hours

Extra time — 2 to 3 days, drying

This delicious confection is also known as Turkish Delight—derived from the Turkish word *lokum*, which in turn comes from the Arabic word for "morsel"— but loukoumi has been adopted by the Greeks as their own sweet treat. This chewy, gummy candy is coated in sugar and can come in a wide variety of flavors, including (but not limited to) orange, pomegranate, almond, and rose.

In *Lore Olympus* fashion, this recipe brings Underworld flavors to the candy by adding lemon, just as Persephone prefers it, to create a sinfully tart and sweet treat.

Loukoumi takes time but is very easy to make and a wonderful addition to an afternoon tea party with the queen of the gods or a holiday gift for friends and family. Refreshing and aromatic, loukoumi is served year-round—usually with a glass of water, tea, or coffee to help cut the sweetness.

---

3 cups (600 g) granulated sugar

3½ cups (825 ml) water, divided

1 teaspoon citric acid

¾ cup (100 g) plus ⅔ cup (80 g) cornstarch, divided

¾ teaspoon cream of tartar

1½ teaspoons lemon extract

1½ cups (190 g) powdered sugar, for coating

1. Line a 9-inch (23 cm) square pan with parchment paper.

2. In a medium-sized heavy saucepan or Dutch oven over medium heat, combine the granulated sugar, 1¼ cups (300 ml) water, and the citric acid. Slowly bring to a boil, stir to dissolve the sugar, and then simmer gently, uncovered and without stirring, until the mixture reaches the soft-ball stage on a candy thermometer (235 to 240 degrees F / 112 to 115 degrees C).

TIP: *Reaching the soft-ball stage is important, as otherwise the loukoumi will be too moist and soak up the powdered sugar mixture at the end. A thermometer is the best way to know if you've reached it, but you can also take a spoonful of the mixture and drop it into a bowl of cold water. Let it cool for a few seconds, then pick it up—if it's pliable and sticky, it has reached the soft-ball stage.*

3. Meanwhile, combine ¾ cup (100 g) cornstarch with the cream of tartar and the remaining 2¼ cups (525 ml) water in a medium-sized heavy saucepan or Dutch oven and place over medium heat. Cook, whisking constantly, until the mixture is homogeneous and thickened. Remove from the heat.

CONTINUED

4. Once the sugar mixture is at the soft-ball stage, gradually pour the sugar mixture into the cornstarch mixture, stirring well. Place over low heat.

5. Cook the mixture, uncovered, over low heat for 1¼ hours, stirring very frequently to prevent sticking. The mixture is ready when it sticks easily to the sides of the pan and takes on a darker, golden color.

6. When the loukoumi mixture is ready, remove from the heat and add the lemon extract. Stir well until combined.

7. Pour the hot mixture into the prepared pan. Set aside to cool. Store uncovered in a cool, dark place for 2 to 3 days, so that the loukoumi can dry out and release any excess moisture.

8. Combine the powdered sugar and ⅔ cup (80 g) cornstarch in a mixing bowl. Dust a cutting board with some of the powdered sugar mixture, then place the loukoumi slab onto the mixture. Dust the surface with additional powdered sugar mixture.

9. Using a large chef's knife dusted with the powdered sugar mixture, cut the loukoumi into squares, dusting the knife with more powdered sugar mixture as needed. Place all the squares into the mixing bowl and thoroughly coat with the powdered sugar mixture. Store in a covered (but not airtight) container, dusting the bottom and top with any remaining powdered sugar mixture.

Minthe, Mint, and the Underworld

Minthe, the scarlet river nymph and former girlfriend of Hades, is one of his few lovers mentioned in mythology. Though Mount Minthi in Elis (where the original Olympic Games were held) is named for Minthe, her name and her myth mainly tie into ancient Greek burial practices. As the story goes, she was transformed into a mint plant by Persephone. Mint was used in funerary practices in ancient Greece to help mask the odor of decay, and it was also a component of the Eleusinian Mystery rites for the worship of Persephone and Demeter.

The Sweet Revenge Pink Cinnamon Rolls

Yield — 12 cinnamon rolls   *Prep time* — 30 minutes   *Cook time* — 25 minutes
Extra time — 1 to 1½ hours, rising

Whether it's in the form of a perfect pink goddess or a delicious dessert, what's not to love about this delectable dish?

Our favorite Dread Queen is referred to by Eros as "the personification of a friggin' cinnamon roll" when he first meets her, and perhaps at first glance this does fit for when she's known as Kore, which is Greek for "maiden" or "girl." The name Persephone, on the other hand, means "bringer of death." The duality of Persephone is what makes her stand apart from so many other goddesses. She is both a perfect cinnamon roll who is too pure for this world and a darkly terrifying gothic queen who is not to be messed with.

And isn't that just so intensely relatable? We are all a little Persephone: delicious, decadent, and dangerous.

FOR THE DOUGH

½ cup (120 ml) warm water
(100 degrees F / 38 degrees C)
1 packet (.25 oz / 7 g) active dry
yeast
1 pinch granulated sugar
2½ cups (315 g) all-purpose flour
1 package (15.25 oz / 430 g)
strawberry cake mix (see note)
¾ cup (180 ml) warm whole milk
(100 degrees F / 38 degrees C)
¼ teaspoon salt
Butter or cooking spray, for
greasing the pan

1. Make the dough: Combine the warm water, yeast, and sugar in a small bowl. Cover with plastic wrap and let sit until foamy, 5 to 10 minutes. If after 10 minutes the mixture isn't substantially foamy, start over with new yeast.

2. Meanwhile, combine the flour, cake mix, warm milk, and salt in a large mixing bowl or the bowl of a stand mixer. Add the yeast mixture and mix together with your hands or, if using a mixer, with the dough hook on low speed. Knead by hand until the dough is smooth and homogeneous, or with the dough hook until the dough comes together and starts to pull away from the sides of the bowl, about 5 minutes.

3. Cover the bowl with plastic wrap and a towel. Let the dough rise in a warm place until almost doubled in size, 1 to 1½ hours.

TIP: *You can preheat the oven to 75 degrees F (25 degrees C), then turn it off and let the dough rise in the oven with the door closed, or use the oven's proofing setting if it has one. The warm temperature helps the dough to rise, though don't let the oven go beyond 110 degrees F (43 degrees C).*

FOR THE FILLING

½ cup (110 g) unsalted butter, softened
½ cup (110 g) brown sugar, packed
½ cup (100 g) granulated sugar
¾ cup (10 g) freeze-dried strawberries, crushed
1 teaspoon vanilla extract
½ teaspoon ground cinnamon

FOR THE ICING

4 oz (110 g) cream cheese, softened
4 oz (110 g) unsalted butter, softened
1½ cups (190 g) powdered sugar
1 teaspoon vanilla extract
2 to 4 tablespoons whole milk, as needed
crushed freeze-dried strawberries, to garnish

COOK'S NOTE: *Don't have strawberry cake mix? You can use any plain cake mix instead, such as a white cake mix or sponge cake mix, and add a few drops of your favorite pink food coloring to the batter. Start with just 1 to 2 drops, as you can always add more to achieve a stronger pink color.*

4. Meanwhile, make the filling: Mix the butter, brown sugar, granulated sugar, freeze-dried strawberries, vanilla, and cinnamon together in a medium bowl until well combined. Grease a 9-by-13-inch (23 by 33 cm) baking pan with butter or cooking spray.

5. Once the dough has doubled in size, remove it from the bowl and place it on a floured work surface. Use a floured rolling pin to roll it into a large rectangle, about 10 by 18 inches (25 by 45 cm). Spread the prepared strawberry filling over the dough, then roll it up into a long log starting from one of the long sides of the rectangle. Slice into 12 rolls and arrange in the prepared pan. Cover with plastic wrap and a towel, and let rise until doubled in size, 45 minutes to 1 hour.

6. Preheat the oven to 375 degrees F (190 degrees C). Bake the rolls in the preheated oven until golden, 20 to 25 minutes. Insert an instant-read thermometer into one of the middle rolls to make sure they are at 190 degrees F (88 degrees C) before removing them from the oven.

7. While the rolls are baking, make the icing: Combine the cream cheese, butter, powdered sugar, and vanilla in a medium mixing bowl. Add 2 tablespoons milk and beat with a whisk or an electric mixer until smooth, adding up to 2 tablespoons more milk until the icing is a thick drizzling consistency.

8. Remove the cinnamon rolls from the oven. Allow to cool slightly before drizzling with the icing and then sprinkling with the freeze-dried strawberries. Serve.

She's like the personification of a friggin' cinnamon roll!

Eros's Apology Donuts

Yield — 6 donuts   *Prep time* — 20 minutes   *Cook time* — 8 minutes

In life and in *Lore Olympus*, you have to take the bitter with the sweet. This is a lesson that Eros, the god of love, learns the hard way after he falls deeply in love with the beautiful mortal princess Psyche and finds himself experiencing heartbreak for the first time.

Spoiler: He does not enjoy it.

On his redemption tour, he becomes friends with Persephone and, having played a cruel prank on her, brings her delicious apology donuts. Because, let's be honest, nothing says "I love you" and "I'm sorry" quite like decadent homemade donuts. Add just a trickle of strawberry glaze to create a simple and delicious dessert—one even a goddess would have a hard time refusing.

FOR THE DONUTS

Butter or cooking spray, for greasing the pan

1 cup (125 g) all-purpose flour

⅓ cup (65 g) granulated sugar

1 teaspoon baking powder

¼ teaspoon salt

¼ cup (50 g) plain Greek yogurt (2 to 5%)

2 tablespoons (30 ml) whole milk

1 tablespoon (15 ml) extra-virgin olive oil

1 teaspoon vanilla extract

zest of 1 lemon

FOR THE GLAZE

1 cup (125 g) powdered sugar, plus more if needed

¼ cup (6 g) freeze-dried strawberries

2 tablespoons (30 ml) whole milk, plus more if needed

1. Make the donuts: Preheat the oven to 425 degrees F (220 degrees C). Grease a donut baking pan with butter or cooking spray.

2. Combine the flour, granulated sugar, baking powder, and salt in a small mixing bowl. In a separate bowl, whisk together the yogurt, milk, olive oil, vanilla, and lemon zest. Add the wet mixture to the dry mixture, stirring until just combined. Spoon evenly into the prepared pan, making six donuts.

> But I have apology donuts!

Eros and Psyche

The tale of Eros and Psyche is one of the few love stories in Greek and Roman mythology with a happy ending. It is also one of the few that feature a female heroine who gets to go on a complete hero's journey, traveling across the classical world and descending into the Underworld, where she meets Persephone.

TIP: *To make things easy, place a plastic food storage bag, one corner down, into a glass. Pour the donut batter into the bag, then remove the bag from the glass and twist the top. Cut a large hole off the corner, then use the bag to pipe the batter into the donut pan.*

3. Bake the donuts in the preheated oven until a tester comes out clean, 7 to 8 minutes. Remove from the pan immediately and let cool.

4. Meanwhile, make the glaze: Grind the powdered sugar and freeze-dried strawberries in a food processor until the strawberries are powdered. Add the milk and process until the glaze is smooth and drizzles easily off a spoon. If the glaze is too thick, add more milk 1 teaspoon at a time; if it's too thin, add more powdered sugar.

5. Once the donuts are cool, spoon the glaze evenly over the top of each donut. Enjoy immediately, or (if you can resist!) let the glaze set before serving.

Strawberry Rose Lemonade

Serves — 6 to 8   *Prep time* — 15 minutes   *Cook time* — 20 minutes

Roses are generally a part of Aphrodite's domain, but there are some roses associated solely with Persephone. The best-preserved examples of Persephone's roses are at Eleusis, the site of the sacred rituals dedicated to Persephone and Demeter that were shrouded in mystery and magic.

This refreshing drink is the essence of that magic, with its dramatic combination of sweet, tart, and floral flavors. Savor it while surveying your lush and verdant kingdom, giving thanks to nature deities, or whenever you need a refreshing pick-me-up.

---

1 cup (240 ml) water

1 cup (200g) granulated sugar

8 oz (225 g) fresh strawberries, hulled and halved, with one to two extra strawberries reserved and sliced for garnish

3 strips lemon peel

1 tablespoon rose water, plus more to taste

1 cup (240 ml) freshly squeezed lemon juice

4 to 6 cups (1 to 1.4 L) water or sparkling water, to taste

COOK'S NOTE: *To turn this drink into a cocktail, serve each glass with 1½ fl oz (45 ml) vodka mixed in.*

1. Combine the water, sugar, strawberries, and lemon peel in a medium saucepan and place over medium-high heat. Bring to a boil, then reduce the heat to medium and simmer gently, uncovered, until the sugar has dissolved and the syrup is a deep red color, 15 to 20 minutes. Don't stir or mash the strawberries, or the syrup will turn cloudy. Remove from the heat, add the rose water, and let cool slightly, 5 to 10 minutes. (See tip.)

2. Carefully pour the contents of the saucepan through a strainer; discard the strawberries and lemon peel, or reserve them for another use. Set the syrup aside to cool completely, or store in the fridge until you're ready to make the lemonade.

3. Combine the syrup, lemon juice, and 4 cups (1 L) water or sparkling water, adding more water to taste. Once you've added water to your liking, taste and add more rose water, if desired. Garnish with the sliced strawberries and serve.

TIP: *You can store the strawberry syrup in the fridge for up to 2 weeks and make individual glasses of lemonade whenever you'd like! To make a single serving, mix 2 tablespoons (15 ml) lemon juice with 2 tablespoons (15 ml) syrup in a tall 16-fl-oz (450 ml) glass. Add ice and top off with water or sparkling water, adding more lemon juice or syrup to taste.*

These are my signature roses…

SUM

A *Celebration* OF
Fertility Goddesses

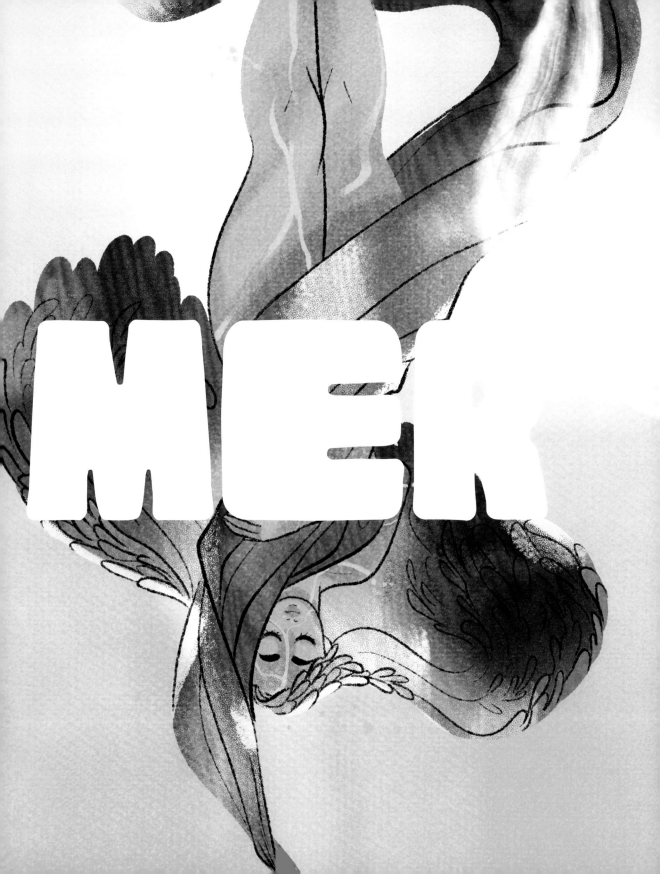

Summer is a time for celebration. It is a time for gathering together with family and friends. For travel and adventure. For enjoying the nice weather, long days, and short nights.

But summer in ancient Greece was a strange time. It was a time when people took a break from their normal lives and celebrated days gone by, a golden age long past. And that golden age belonged to . . . Kronos.

Yes, the villain of *Lore Olympus* was fêted every summer by the ancient Greeks in a festival called the Kronia. The Kronia was supposed to commemorate the reign of Kronos, when it was believed that the world was always warm and food and resources were plentiful.

During the festival, the fabric of Greek society was upended. Women and men could dine together. Enslaved people were given the day off and allowed to eat at banquets and move freely throughout the city. Social hierarchy melted away, harkening back to the time of Kronos, when there was equality for all.

Of course, the ancient Greeks also believed that Kronos was a tyrant.

So how did an oppressor usher in a golden age? The answer is one that *Lore Olympus* posits over and over again: fertility goddesses.

What is the role of a fertility goddess? They are common across cultures around the globe. You can find figures like Persephone, Gaia, and Metis scattered throughout many other mythologies.

In the world of *Lore Olympus,* fertility goddesses were imbued with immense power. Their role was to nourish the earth, grow and create new things, and serve as a counter to male gods (who tended to get a little power-crazy and sometimes eat their children—looking at you, Kronos). When fertility goddesses

were in harmony with their partners, they could create new worlds together; Hades and Persephone repair the Underworld, create the Elysian Fields, and defeat Kronos. But when the two partners are not united, when a male god tries to use a fertility goddess's powers for himself, the ending is always the destruction of the greedy god. Even if it takes a few millennia for the god to get his comeuppance.

Summer is a time of harmony. It's a time of warmth and growth and celebration. Since ancient times, summer has been a season for coming together. And in this season's recipes we share different dishes that will be sure to please crowds. Cold mezes for scorching hot days. Refreshing drinks for sizzling nights. All of these dishes are designed to be cooked and shared during the summer. Whether you're looking to impress at your next barbecue or preparing a week's worth of innovative lunches for work, channeling the powers of the ancient fertility goddesses will help you to eat and live more seasonably.

Strapatsada

Serves — 4   *Prep time* — 5 minutes   *Cook time* — 20 minutes

Strapatsada is a popular summer meal in Greece—a delicious scramble of eggs, feta, and fresh tomatoes. It is simple to make, can be served hot or cold, and uses fresh seasonal ingredients.

This dish is so tasty and easy to make that it elevates the traditional scrambled eggs on toast to a new level. Usually served with crusty bread, it is the best way to start your morning, especially if you're coming out of a stressful evening—like if you had to do battle with a tyrannical Titan, for example. Or at least, that's exactly what Hestia and Amphitrite thought when they made this breakfast for Persephone and Hades just before they whisked Persephone away for a much-deserved spa day after the defeat of Kronos.

½ medium red onion

¼ cup (60 ml) extra-virgin olive oil

1 can (28 oz / 800 g) peeled whole tomatoes, such as San Marzano (see tip)

½ teaspoon salt

½ teaspoon dried Greek oregano

1 pinch granulated sugar

1 cup (7g) loosely packed mint leaves

1 cup (7g) loosely packed flat-leaf parsley

salt and pepper, to taste

8 large eggs, lightly beaten

4 oz (110 g) sheep's-milk feta cheese, crumbled, plus extra to garnish

crushed red chile pepper flakes or Aleppo pepper flakes, for serving (optional)

1. Using the large holes of a box grater, grate the red onion until you have ½ cup grated onion (approximately 100 g).

2. Heat the olive oil in a large frying pan over medium heat. Add the grated onion and cook gently until softened, 3 to 5 minutes.

3. Add the tomatoes to the frying pan along with the salt, oregano, and sugar. Using a potato masher or fork, gently mash the tomatoes until they've broken apart. Bring the mixture to a simmer and cook gently until the tomato sauce has thickened and any excess liquid has evaporated, 8 to 10 minutes. During the last couple of minutes, stir in the mint and parsley, then season with salt and pepper.

4. Season the beaten eggs with salt and pepper and whisk until combined. Add the eggs and feta to the tomato mixture, gently stirring through, but taking care not to fully incorporate the eggs—you want some larger bits of egg in the sauce. Continue to cook gently over medium heat, stirring occasionally, until the eggs are set and cooked through, about 5 minutes.

CONTINUED

5. Serve garnished with more feta crumbled over the top and a sprinkle of crushed red chile pepper if you like some heat!

TIP: *When tomatoes are ripe, juicy, and in season, you can make this dish with fresh tomatoes. Use approximately 2 lb (900 g) large tomatoes; cut them in half and grate on the large holes of a box grater, discarding the skin. Follow the recipe from step 2, allowing more time for the sauce to reduce. Add 1 to 2 tablespoons tomato paste to help thicken the sauce, if desired.*

Poseidon's Kitty-Shaped Pancakes

Yield — **4 to 6 pancakes**   *Prep time* — **15 minutes**   *Cook time* — **20 minutes**

In Episode 84 of *Lore Olympus*, aptly named "Pancakes," Poseidon and Zeus crash Hades's home for a brothers brunch to dissect the King of the Underworld's evening with Persephone. Poseidon makes an almighty mess in the perfectly organized kitchen as he whips up kitty-shaped buttermilk pancakes from scratch and sprinkles in some surprisingly sage wisdom on relationships. It's his party trick: wrecking the kitchen, offering unexpected insights, and flawlessly flipping pancakes.

Garnish this showstopping brunch treat with fresh berries, maple syrup, chocolate chips, fresh whipped cream, and wise counsel to any besties or siblings who clearly need it.

And don't forget—never take romantic advice from Zeus.

---

1 cup (240 ml) plus 2 tablespoons (30 ml) whole milk, divided
1 tablespoon apple cider vinegar
1 cup (125 g) all-purpose flour
2 tablespoons granulated sugar
1 teaspoon baking powder
½ teaspoon baking soda
¼ teaspoon salt
2 tablespoons (30 g) butter, melted
1 egg
1 tablespoon unsweetened cocoa powder
1 teaspoon vanilla extract

1. Combine ¾ cup (180 ml) milk with the vinegar and let sit while you prepare the dry ingredients.

2. Combine the flour, sugar, baking powder, baking soda, and salt in a large mixing bowl.

3. Add the melted butter and egg to the milk-vinegar mixture and whisk well. Add to the dry ingredients and fold together until just combined and no dry spots remain.

4. Remove ½ cup (150 g) of the pancake batter and place in a small bowl. To this smaller amount of batter, add the cocoa powder and 2 tablespoons (30 ml) milk. Stir until combined and pour into a plastic squeeze bottle.

5. To the remaining plain batter, add the vanilla and ¼ cup (60 ml) milk. Whisk until smooth.

6. Heat a lightly greased large frying pan over medium-high heat. Using the squeeze bottle, draw an outline of a cat's face with the chocolate batter. Draw whiskers in the center and add a dot for the nose. Let the chocolate

CONTINUED

COOK'S NOTE: *You'll need a squeeze bottle for the chocolate pancake batter to make the kitty outline and whiskers. Use a store-bought squeeze bottle and snip off the end to make the hole slightly larger and easier for the pancake batter to flow. Alternatively, you can use a repurposed plastic bottle, such as a clean ketchup bottle.*

batter set for 15 to 30 seconds, then ladle in the vanilla batter, covering the whiskers and nose and coming up to the edges of the outline. Cook until bubbles appear on the surface of the vanilla batter, 2 to 3 minutes, then carefully flip. Cook the other side until golden, 1 to 2 minutes more.

7. Repeat with the remaining batter, making 4 to 6 pancakes in total.

TIP: *It works best if you use a large frying pan and make one pancake at a time. Start by outlining the first ear, coming down into a full circle and up to the second ear, ending where you started with the first ear. The whiskers can be tricky to get at first, but three on the left and three on the right, with a dot in the middle for the nose, works best!*

Greek Freddo

Serves — 1   *Prep time* — 5 minutes

When the temperature rises there is nothing as refreshing as freddo, or Greek iced coffee.

Freddo is a favorite of *Lore Olympus*'s resident coffee snob, Hades. While it won't be invented in the *Lore Olympus* mortal realm for quite a while, you can bet that Hades has his own regular coffee shop and freddo order on standby in the Underworld.

Delicious and easy to make, this is the morning pick-me-up drink that defines the long hot summers in Greece today. Available in every cafe, taverna, or bakery, this double shot of espresso on ice, a top layer of cold milk foam, and a little bit of sugar brings some much-needed chill to summer days.

FOR THE FREDDO ESPRESSO

2 shots espresso (2 fl oz / 60 ml)
sugar, to taste (optional) (see note)

FOR THE FREDDO CAPPUCCINO

2 to 3 tablespoons skim milk, to
    taste, well chilled
2 shots espresso (2 fl oz / 60 ml)
sugar, to taste (optional)
cocoa powder or ground
    cinnamon, to garnish
    (optional)

You don't want coffee, sweetheart.

FOR THE FREDDO ESPRESSO

1. Brew two shots of espresso. Stir in the sugar, if desired.

2. Froth the espresso by adding it to a cocktail shaker with 5 or 6 ice cubes. Close the lid and shake well, 20 to 30 seconds. Remove the lid and pour into a glass to serve, adding more ice if you like.

3. Alternatively, if you do not have a cocktail shaker, place the espresso and ice cubes in a large jar or glass. Froth with a milk frother to make a thick foam. Pour into a serving glass with additional ice.

FOR THE FREDDO CAPPUCCINO

1. Place the milk in a glass jar. Use a milk frother to froth the milk until doubled in volume, 2 to 3 minutes. Skim milk works better than any other dairy or nondairy milk for frothing, and it should be very cold for best results.

2. Brew two shots of espresso. Stir in the sugar, if desired. Pour the espresso over a tall glass full of ice. Top with the foamed milk, spooning it over the top and not stirring so that the layers remain distinct. If desired, lightly dust the foam with cocoa powder.

COOK'S NOTE: *You can take your freddo* sketo *(no sugar),* metrio *(medium sweet), or* glyko *(sweet). If you do take sugar, be sure to stir it into the espresso until dissolved before adding the ice.*

Morpheus's Sweet Dreams Mocktail

Serves — 2   *Prep time* — 5 minutes

A good night's sleep makes all the difference. And who better to help you find your sleepy bliss than the blue-winged goddess of dreams herself, Morpheus? She's always by your side, helping you navigate the shifting landscape of your dreams.

Whether you're stressed out after a busy day at work, a big exam, or family and relationship drama, Morpheus is here for you. This tart cherry and honey mocktail is a delicious addition to your nighttime self-care routine. Use it to help you unwind and relax—or you can add some vodka and turn it into a cocktail, for those nights when partying is on the menu before sleep.

Just don't stay up too late.

---

1 tablespoon honey

2 tablespoons hot water

½ cup (120 ml) 100% tart cherry juice

1 tablespoon lime juice

2 to 3 fresh basil leaves, to taste, plus extra to garnish

⅔ cup (150 ml) sparkling water

COOK'S NOTE: *Instead of basil, you can try a sprig of rosemary for a different herbaceous twist.*

1. Place the honey and hot water in a cocktail shaker and stir until the honey is dissolved. You can instead use 3 tablespoons of the honey syrup from the Warming Winter Ambrosia on page 193.

2. Pour the cherry juice and lime juice into the cocktail shaker and add the basil. Fill with ice. Cover and shake until the outside of the shaker is frosty, 20 to 30 seconds.

3. Strain the mixture into two glasses and top with the sparkling water. Add ice, garnish with basil leaves, and serve.

TIP: *Make this a cocktail by adding 1½ fl oz (45 ml) vodka or mastiha, a Greek liqueur, per serving.*

Morpheus and Dreams
Morpheus is the goddess of dreams. She is transgender, and she makes her first appearance in Episode 201 of *Lore Olympus*. Because of her ability to live on the edge of dreams and waking, she is initially not affected by Kronos's time manipulation powers and is able to help Persephone take down the dreaded Titan.

Briam

Serves — 4   *Prep time* — 25 minutes   *Cook time* — 1½ to 1¾ hours

Demeter is the goddess of the harvest. In *Lore Olympus*, Persephone imagines her and the nymphs working hard every day—caring for the plants and ensuring that there will be a good harvest for the mortals. She has a pang of homesickness, missing her family and their sit-down dinners of briam—or slow-baked summer vegetables—made with the bounty from their garden when the workday is done.

This briam re-creates Persephone's family recipe, utilizing fresh summer vegetables like green beans, tomatoes, and zucchini, along with potatoes and red onion. While you will need the same level of patience and dedication that Demeter employs to ensure that the mortal realm flourishes, it is worth the wait to create this delectable cornucopia of flavor.

---

1 lb (450 g) zucchini (3 medium), trimmed

1 lb (450 g) yellow potatoes (2 large), peeled

1 large red onion

1 bell pepper (any color), cored

8 oz (225 g) green beans, trimmed

1½ cups tomato pulp (see tip)

1 teaspoon salt, or to taste

pepper, to taste

½ cup (120 ml) extra-virgin olive oil

1. Preheat the oven to 400 degrees F (200 degrees C).

2. Prepare the vegetables: Slice the zucchini, potatoes, and onion into thin rounds, between ⅛ and ¼ inch (3–6 mm) thick. Cut the bell pepper into 1-inch (2.5 cm) pieces. Place in a 15-by-10-inch (38 by 25 cm) roasting pan along with the green beans, tomato, salt, pepper, and olive oil. Stir to coat.

3. Bake in the preheated oven for 1 hour. Check the vegetables and stir gently, then add up to ¼ cup (60 ml) water if the vegetables are too dry. Return to the oven and bake until the vegetables are soft, wrinkly, and charred in spots, and there is only oil left in the pan, 30 to 45 minutes. Resist the urge to stir the vegetables often while baking, as this will break up the starch in the potato and alter the texture of the dish. Also avoid adding too much water, as there should be no liquid left at the end of baking.

4. Remove from the oven and allow to cool slightly. Serve warm or at room temperature.

TIP: *The classic Greek style of preparing tomatoes for dishes like this is to cut a large tomato in half, then grate the tomato cut side down on the large holes of a box grater, discarding the skin. You'll need 4 to 5 large tomatoes if you go this route, but you can easily use canned chopped tomatoes in a pinch.*

Shrimp Saganaki

Serves — 4   *Prep time* — 10 minutes   *Cook time* — 25 minutes

Shrimp have always been on the menu in Greece. There are four species of shrimp that are native to the Mediterranean, and you can see them depicted in ancient artwork, paintings, pottery, and writing. In fact, there is a Greek deity of shrimp, Nerites. There are several different versions of Nerites's mythology: He was a lover of either Aphrodite or Poseidon, and was turned into a shrimp and made the god of shellfish.

Shrimp Saganaki is a cheesy, tomatoey dish that can be a part of a meze board or a full meal (just add a side salad and rice or small pasta such as orzo). Incredibly easy to cook, this is the type of meal that quickly becomes a fast and delicious go-to for any occasion.

¼ cup (60 ml) extra-virgin olive oil

1 small red onion, grated on the large holes of a box grater

¼ cup (60 ml) ouzo (see tip)

18 oz (500 g) canned whole plum tomatoes, mashed

2 tablespoons finely chopped fresh parsley

2 tablespoons finely chopped fresh mint

salt and pepper, to taste

12 oz (350 g) large shrimp, peeled and deveined

7 oz (200 g) sheep's-milk feta cheese, crumbled

crusty bread, for serving

1. Heat the olive oil in a large sauté pan over medium heat and add the onion. Cook gently until softened but not browned, about 5 minutes. Increase the heat to medium high, then add the ouzo. Simmer until the alcohol burns off, 1 to 2 minutes, then add the tomatoes, parsley, mint, and salt and pepper. Bring to a simmer, then reduce the heat to medium and simmer gently, uncovered, until the sauce is thickened, 10 to 15 minutes.

2. Season the shrimp with salt and pepper, then add to the sauce, turning the heat up to medium high. Cook the shrimp until they start to turn opaque, 1 to 2 minutes, then flip the shrimp over and crumble the feta evenly over the top. Continue to cook until the shrimp are pink, opaque, and cooked through, 2 to 3 minutes more. Serve straightaway with lots of good, crusty bread.

TIP: *If you don't have ouzo, you can use white wine or even vodka. And if you like a bit of heat, try sprinkling with crushed red chile flakes or Aleppo pepper flakes just before serving.*

White Bean Tuna Salad

Serves — 6   *Prep time* — 15 minutes

Tuna is incredibly versatile and multifaceted—much like Amphitrite, wife of Poseidon and queen of the sea.

Amphitrite is a sea goddess who has spent her life weathering raging storms, fierce waves, and wild waters. She is one of the fifty Nereids—daughters of the ancient sea deities Nereus and Doris—and sister of Thetis. Myth tells us that Poseidon fell in love with Amphitrite at first sight, which would normally be the end of this swoon-worthy tale. But Poseidon and Amphitrite were both as changeable as the sea, and would fall in and out of love (and lust) with each other.

In *Lore Olympus*, Amphitrite is happily in a polyamorous relationship with her husband, allowing them both the freedom they crave. And though both of these rulers are like the sea—tempestuous and unpredictable—their love is as constant as the tides. This combination works together to create an unbreakable relationship in Greek mythology.

Another combination that works together flawlessly? Tuna and white beans. The two blend together to create an out-of-this-world taste—both passionate and a little stormy.

---

2 cans (5 oz / 142 g each) yellowfin tuna in water, drained

2 cans (15 oz / 425 g each) cannellini beans, drained

⅔ cup (40 g) chopped fresh flat-leaf parsley

⅓ cup (20 g) chopped fresh mint

1 shallot, thinly sliced into rounds

1 jarred roasted red pepper, finely chopped

3 tablespoons extra-virgin olive oil

2 tablespoons lemon juice

½ teaspoon salt, or to taste (see tip)

pepper, to taste

3 cups spring mix, mizuna, or other greens

1. In a large mixing bowl, combine the tuna, beans, parsley, mint, shallot, roasted red pepper, olive oil, lemon juice, salt, and pepper. Gently stir until well combined; the starchiness from the beans will help bring everything together.

TIP: *Be careful with the salt! The amount you add to the salad will depend on whether your tuna and beans came packed with salt added.*

2. To serve, place a bed of greens on a large serving platter or on individual plates, then top with the tuna mixture. Though it is best served immediately, the leftovers will keep in the fridge for up to 3 days.

Caramelized Figs with Ice Cream

Serves — 4 to 6   *Prep time* — 10 minutes   *Cook time* — 15 minutes

Figs have been considered a delicacy since the dawn of time. While they were not native to Greece, they were successfully cultivated and domesticated there, becoming a staple of the ancient diet. In fact, the Greek lawmaker Solon (circa 630–560 B.C.E.) passed a law forbidding the export of figs from Greece, and the theft of figs was considered a crime. Figs are so numerous in Greece now that from late August into September you can find trees overflowing with the fruit.

Figs were considered a sign of wisdom, success, and abundance. Mythologically they were tied to Dionysus and Aphrodite: According to one myth, figs were created by Aphrodite's tears, and in ancient times they were used in some wines and to make souma, which forged their connection to Dionysus.

Caramelized figs are a simple and showstopping dessert; filled with the intoxicating flavors of summer, they truly are a gift from the gods.

---

4 tablespoons pine nuts (see tip)
¾ cup (150 g) granulated sugar
2 tablespoons water
1 tablespoon lemon juice
½ vanilla bean, split lengthwise
12 mission figs, trimmed and cut
    in half
vanilla ice cream, for serving

1. Place the pine nuts in a small frying pan over medium heat. Cook, stirring frequently, until golden all over, 4 to 5 minutes. Remove from the heat.

TIP: *Almonds, pecans, or hazelnuts also work well if you don't have pine nuts.*

2. Place the sugar, water, lemon juice, and vanilla bean in a large sauté or frying pan over medium heat. Cook until the sugar is dissolved and the mixture is syrupy, 3 to 5 minutes.

3. Add the figs to the pan, cut sides down, and cook undisturbed, until soft and caramelized, 5 to 7 minutes. Remove the figs from the pan to serving bowls, allotting 4 to 6 fig halves per person. Serve with a scoop of vanilla ice cream, caramel sauce from the pan spooned on top, and a sprinkling of toasted pine nuts.

Horiatiki

Serves — 4   *Prep time* — 10 minutes   *Extra time* — 20 minutes, marinating

Horiatiki—also known as Greek salad or village salad—is on every menu in Greece. It is also the type of meal you can imagine Demeter's nymphs putting together on a hot summer's evening, the vegetables still warm from the sun. Traditional Greek cuisine is focused on fresh, seasonal ingredients, and horiatiki is usually served in summer, when the vegetables are all in season.

    This dish is also a study of contrasts—salty olives, creamy feta, sweet tomatoes, sharp red onion—much like our beloved Persephone. So embrace the full suite of flavors in this delicious meal that, at first glance, is just a simple village salad—but, when everything comes together, is actually a magnificent feast fit for a queen.

---

5 large tomatoes

1½ teaspoons dried Greek oregano

salt, to taste

1 small green bell pepper, sliced

½ small red onion, thinly sliced

½ medium cucumber, sliced

1 handful Kalamata olives

1 slice (7 oz / 200 g) sheep's-milk
    feta cheese

3 tablespoons extra-virgin
    olive oil

1. Cut the tomatoes into wedges, working over a large serving bowl so that any extra juices land in the bowl. Add the oregano, then season liberally with salt; stir well. Let the tomatoes sit at room temperature until their juices have released, at least 20 minutes.

2. Mix in the bell pepper, onion, cucumber, and olives just before serving. Top with the feta cheese and drizzle with the olive oil.

Artemis's Broken Phyllo Cherry Ice Cream Cake

Serves — 6 to 8   *Prep time* — 30 minutes   *Cook time* — 15 minutes   *Extra time* — 8 hours, freezing

Artemis and Persephone's friendship is one of the most unlikely in the world of *Lore Olympus*. Artemis is usually a loner, but she genuinely cares about Persephone, even if they sometimes don't communicate as well as they should.

And never is that more apparent than when Artemis (not a talented baker) tries to make Persephone (an extremely talented baker) an apology cake. It turns out about as well as you'd imagine.

Drawing inspiration from that moment, this delicious cherry ice cream cake emulates the friendship between Artemis and Persephone; it has rough edges with its broken phyllo pastry, but is ultimately sweet and wonderful.

FOR THE BROKEN PHYLLO

2 tablespoons butter, melted
4 sheets phyllo (see note)
1½ tablespoons granulated sugar

FOR THE ICE CREAM

1 pint (470 ml) heavy whipping cream, chilled
1 can (14 oz / 397 g) sweetened condensed milk
1 tablespoon Cointreau (see tip)
1 pinch salt
1 cup (225 g) Amarena cherries or Greek sour cherry spoon sweet (vyssino)

1. Make the broken phyllo: Brush a baking sheet with melted butter and lay a sheet of phyllo on top. Brush the phyllo sheet with butter, then lay a second sheet on top. Continue layering, brushing each sheet with butter, until all the sheets are stacked on top of one another. Finish by brushing the top of the final sheet with butter and sprinkling evenly with the sugar. Place in the fridge until the butter has resolidified, 5 to 10 minutes.

2. Preheat the oven to 375 degrees F (190 degrees C). Line a 9-by-5-inch (23 by 13 cm) loaf pan with parchment paper with plenty of overhang.

3. Remove the phyllo from the fridge and transfer to the oven. Bake until crispy and a deep golden brown, 10 to 15 minutes. Set aside to cool.

4. Make the ice cream: Beat the heavy whipping cream with an electric mixer until stiff peaks form, about 4 minutes. Add the condensed milk, Cointreau, and salt and gently fold together until no streaks remain.

TIP: *If you don't have Cointreau, try using brandy or Metaxa. You can also skip the alcohol entirely and use 1 teaspoon vanilla extract instead.*

CONTINUED

5. Break the cooled phyllo with your hands into small pieces roughly ½ inch (12 mm) in size.

6. Sprinkle a thin, even layer of phyllo on the bottom of the prepared loaf pan. Dot with about a third of the cherries. Cover with about a third of the cream mixture. Repeat the layers, ending with a cream layer.

7. Place the pan in the freezer and freeze for 8 hours or overnight.

8. When ready to serve, invert the pan on a serving platter or cutting board and carefully remove the parchment paper. Slice the cake and garnish each serving with extra broken phyllo.

YOUR
VERY OWN

Summer UNDER-WORLD BARBECUE Feast

Souvlaki
pg 102

Huntress
Pita Bread
pg 98

Tzatziki
pg 97

Watermelon
Margarita
pg 104

Spicy Roasted
Red Pepper
and Feta Dip
pg 94

Our summer feast is based on the epic mortal-realm-meets-Underworld barbecue scenes in Episode 156, "Cow," and Episode 157, "Hypothetical." This moment in *Lore Olympus* history marks the first time that Persephone's family (except for Demeter, who is MIA) officially meet Hades. After trashing his house, building a fire pit, taking over his swimming pool, and shamelessly ogling the hunky god, the nymphs overwhelmingly approve of the King of the Underworld!

Hades, in turn, very much enjoys Persephone's eccentric and outgoing family. He is genuinely pleased that Persephone's relatives are so happy and at home visiting the Underworld, and that his big, normally empty house is filled with laughter and love. The party ends with Hades and Persephone dancing for their guests. It is the first time the couple have danced in public, and they light up the Underworld with their joy while the nymphs laugh and cheer around them. Filled with family, festivities, and food, it is a bright spot in an otherwise dark time for Persephone.

In that spirit of joy and celebration, we've created this summer feast to be a crowd-pleaser, with recipes to create a perfect meze board, cocktails to dazzle your guests, and a chicken souvlaki recipe so tender that you will never want to eat anything else.

Spicy Roasted Red Pepper and Feta Dip

Serves — 6   *Prep time* — 10 minutes

Meze boards are a huge part of the Greek diet. Greeks make an entire meal out of disparate dishes, allowing for small bites and varied flavors. In ancient times, meat was reserved for the wealthy (or special feast days), and so it often wasn't a part of daily life. Instead, complex and delicious flavors were created from local in-season vegetables, cheeses, and fruits. Many daily meals would be vegetarian, something Persephone heartily approves of.

Perhaps one of the most popular additions to any Greek meze board is the spicy roasted red pepper and feta dip known as tyrokafteri—which literally translates to "spicy cheese." When you mix the salty sweetness of feta with spicy roasted red peppers, you get a dip that would have pride of place at Persephone's Underworld family barbecue.

---

11 oz (300 g) sheep's-milk feta cheese, divided

1 jarred roasted red pepper

½ cup (100 g) plain Greek yogurt (2 to 5%)

2 tablespoons extra-virgin olive oil

1 tablespoon Aleppo pepper flakes or 1 teaspoon crushed red chile pepper flakes, plus more to taste

1. Combine half of the feta with the roasted red pepper, yogurt, olive oil, and Aleppo pepper in a food processor or blender. Process until smooth and homogeneous, about 1 minute.

2. Meanwhile, crumble the remaining feta in a medium bowl or container. Add the red pepper mixture and stir to combine. Taste and add more Aleppo pepper to increase the heat level, if desired. Serve immediately or place in the refrigerator for 1 to 2 hours for a thicker texture.

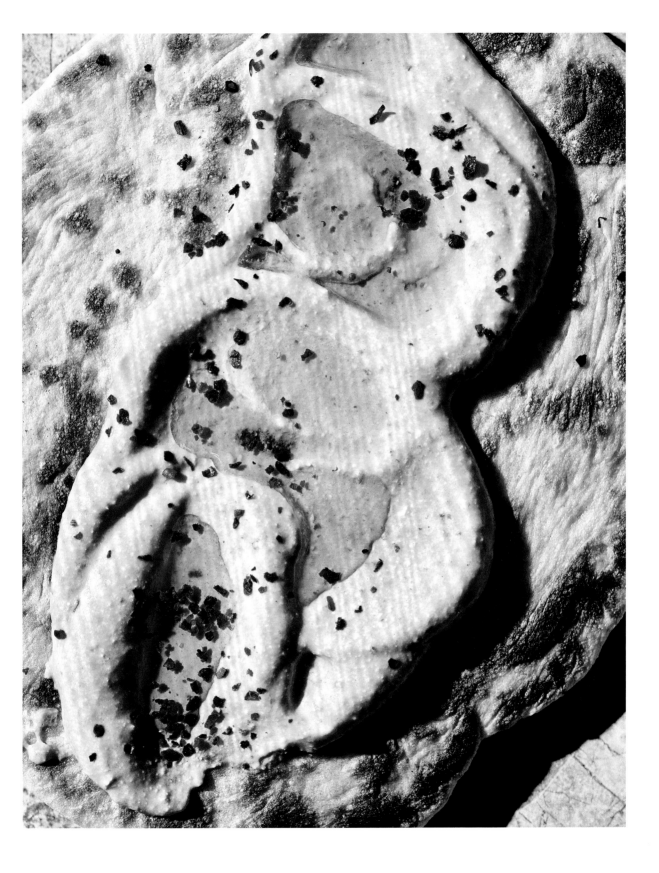

Tzatziki

Serves — **6 to 8**   *Prep time* — **20 minutes**

Tzatziki is *the* taste of summer. Made from cucumbers and Greek yogurt, this dip can be served as part of a meze board with vegetables and fresh pita bread, with souvlaki and gyros, or with salad. It is wildly versatile and so simple to make at home.

The ancient Greek word for cucumbers is *angoúri*, meaning "unripe"—they were usually harvested early and then left to ripen at home. They were also protected by the ancient Greek and Roman god Priapus, who (hilariously) was always depicted as being naked with a very large . . . eggplant emoji. He was a fertility god, a brother (or sometimes son) of Dionysus, and the god of vegetables and produce—and he took his protection of produce very seriously.

¼ cup (60 ml) extra-virgin olive oil

2 tablespoons (30 ml) red wine vinegar

1 to 2 cloves garlic, to taste, minced

1 English cucumber, peeled

16 oz (450 g) plain Greek yogurt (2 to 5%)

salt, to taste

1. Combine the olive oil, vinegar, and garlic in a mixing bowl. Set aside.

2. Halve the cucumber lengthwise and scoop out the seeds. Grate the cucumber on the large holes of a box grater. Place in the center of a clean tea towel, then gather the towel into a pouch and squeeze out as much cucumber liquid as possible.

3. Add the squeezed cucumber and yogurt to the oil mixture. Stir until thoroughly combined, then season with salt. Serve immediately or store in the refrigerator for up to 5 days.

Huntress Pita Bread

Yield — 6 pita breads   *Prep time* — 15 minutes   *Cook time* — 35 minutes
Extra time — 40 minutes, rising

Finally, a pita bread recipe so easy even Artemis could get it right.

The goddess of the hunt has a lot of talents—but baking isn't one of them. She's much more at home in the forests and fields than in the kitchen, but when she's off on a hunting trip, she needs a simple form of sustenance that is easy to make.

Enter this delicious pita bread, perfect for beginning bakers or people with limited time (and counter space!). Greek pita bread is soft and fluffy and doesn't have a pocket, and we suggest pairing it with our homemade tzatziki (page 97).

3 cups (375 g) all-purpose flour

1 packet (.25 oz / 7 g) instant yeast (2¼ teaspoons) (see note)

1 teaspoon granulated sugar

½ teaspoon salt

¾ cup (180 ml) warm water (125 degrees F / 50 degrees C)

½ cup (120 ml) warm whole milk (100 degrees F / 38 degrees C)

1 tablespoon extra-virgin olive oil, plus extra for greasing your hands and the dough balls

COOK'S NOTE: *If you don't have instant yeast, you can use regular active dry yeast—just be sure to proof it first with lukewarm water (100 degrees F / 38 degrees C) and sugar until foamy, 5 to 10 minutes, then add the yeast mixture to the remaining ingredients.*

1. Stir together the flour, yeast, sugar, and salt in the bowl of a stand mixer. Add the water, milk, and olive oil and mix with the dough hook attachment until the dough no longer sticks to the sides, about 6 minutes.

TIP: *If you don't have a stand mixer, start kneading the dough in a large mixing bowl until it comes together, then transfer it to a work surface and continue kneading for about 6 minutes. Resist the urge to add more flour or overknead; the dough will become less sticky as you go.*

2. Cover the dough with plastic wrap and let it rise in a warm place until doubled in size, about 20 minutes.

3. Remove the dough from the bowl and roll into a thick log. Cut into 6 equal pieces. Gently knead and roll each piece into a ball. Let the balls rise for 15 to 20 minutes.

4. Lightly grease your hands and the outside of a dough ball with olive oil. Using your hands, stretch the ball into a circle. Begin stretching and turning the dough in your hands, then lay it flat on a work surface and use your fingers to stretch it into a circle approximately 6 to 7 inches (15 to 18 cm) in diameter and no more than ¼ inch (6 mm) thick. Finally, poke the dough with your fingers to create light dimples all over the surface. Repeat with the remaining dough balls.

Protector of the Young

In addition to being the goddess of the hunt, Artemis was also the protector of the young. Infant and child mortality rates were high in the ancient world, so it was important to have a goddess who looked after children as they grew. Once they reached adulthood, people would leave offerings of their childhood toys or clothes on her altars.

5. Heat a cast-iron or nonstick frying pan over medium heat. Set a glass of water and a teaspoon to the side of the stove. Once the pan is hot, quickly add the first pita, then sprinkle 1 teaspoon water around the edge of the pan. Cover with a lid to trap the steam, which will help ensure fluffiness. Cook for 2 to 3 minutes, then flip and cook for 1 to 2 minutes more. Both sides should have golden brown spots all over. Remove the pita to a plate and cover with a tea towel. Repeat with the remaining dough.

Souvlaki

Serves — 6   *Prep time* — 20 minutes   *Cook time* — 15 minutes (souvlaki), 50 to 70 minutes (gyros)
Extra time — 1 hour, marinating

Want to upgrade your summer barbecue? Souvlaki is the crowd-pleasing Greek version. You can make this succulent chicken dish on a grill or in the oven. Healthy and hearty, souvlaki is a meal you'll want to eat again and again all summer. And it even tastes great cold!

Souvlaki feels very modern, but it's actually ancient—Aristotle and Aristophanes even shared recipes for souvlaki! The most ancient Greek souvlaki wouldn't have been made with chicken, but rather with pork, lamb, or other meats. Archeologists have uncovered evidence on the island of Santorini of souvlaki-like cooking dating back to the seventeenth century B.C.E., as they've found stone cooking tools preserved by the volcanic eruption of Thera—ancient Greece's even more ancient version of Pompeii.

In *Lore Olympus*, Persephone's family from the mortal realm invite themselves over to Hades's house for an impromptu party. When they find that the King of the Underworld has no fire pit, they build one so that they can cook souvlaki and roast vegetables. It is a joyous and chaotic reunion—complete with good food and lots of dancing.

FOR THE SOUVLAKI OR GYROS

4 tablespoons extra-virgin olive oil, plus extra for oiling the grill

2 large garlic cloves, minced

2 teaspoons salt

2 teaspoons sweet paprika

2 teaspoons sumac

1½ teaspoons dried Greek oregano

pepper, to taste

2½ lb (1.3 kg) boneless, skinless chicken thighs

In a large mixing bowl or resealable plastic bag, combine the olive oil, garlic, salt, paprika, sumac, oregano, and pepper. Mix well. Add the chicken thighs and coat on all sides. Cover the bowl or seal the bag, then transfer to the fridge to marinate for 1 hour or overnight.

TO PREPARE SOUVLAKI

1. Soak 8 to 12 bamboo skewers in water to prevent burning on the grill.

2. Preheat an outdoor grill to medium-high heat and lightly oil the grate.

3. Using kitchen shears, cut the marinated chicken thighs into approximately 1-inch (2.5 cm) cubes. Thread the chicken pieces onto the skewers.

6 pita breads

tzatziki (page 97)

1 red onion, sliced

1 to 2 tomatoes, cut into thin
    wedges

COOK'S NOTE: *If you have a grill,
you can follow the recipe to make juicy
and succulent chicken souvlaki skewers.
If you don't have a grill, you can use
all of the same ingredients to make loaf
pan chicken gyros.*

4. Place the skewers on the preheated grill and cook until the meat no longer sticks and the skewer easily releases from the grate, about 2 minutes. Continue to cook, turning frequently, until the chicken is browned on all sides and no longer pink in the center, 10 to 12 minutes.

TO PREPARE GYROS

1. Preheat the oven to 350 degrees F (180 degrees C) and line a 9-by-5-inch (23 by 13 cm) loaf pan with a large sheet of parchment paper with plenty of overhang.

2. Layer the chicken thighs in the loaf pan, staggering the layers so that the thighs are overlapping slightly. Press down on each layer before starting another and press down on the final layer, so that the chicken is tightly packed.

TIP: *To keep the chicken in place, stick four to six toothpicks or bamboo skewers through the layers until they reach the bottom of the pan. If using skewers, break off the tops of the skewers just above the chicken.*

3. Bake in the preheated oven until the center of the loaf is 165 degrees F (74 degrees C), 60 to 70 minutes.

4. Remove the pan from the oven and let rest for 5 to 10 minutes.

5. Pour off the accumulated juices in the pan and set aside. Carefully lift out the loaf and place on a large platter or cutting board. Remove the toothpicks at one end and slice crosswise with a sharp knife. Continue slicing until you've reached the end of the loaf. Spoon 2 to 3 tablespoons of the reserved juices over the sliced chicken to moisten.

TO SERVE

Serve the chicken souvlaki or gyros wrapped in pita with tzatziki, sliced red onion, and tomato wedges. Alternatively, serve as a platter with pita triangles and the tzatziki, red onion, and tomato on the side.

Watermelon Margarita

Serves — **1 to 6**   *Prep time* — **15 minutes**

Watermelon has long been associated with summer. By the first century B.C.E. the watermelon had reached ancient Greece. Initially, this fruit was bitter and used for practical purposes, such as for curing heatstroke by placing a watermelon rind on the forehead, as a diuretic, and even as a vessel for transporting liquid! The fruit was so dense with water that it acted as a natural canteen, and many ships would use watermelons both for trade purposes and to carry water for the crew during long voyages at sea. That is why the watermelon spread so quickly around the globe.

The bitter taste of watermelon was soon bred out of the fruit (around 200 C.E.), leaving behind the sweet and refreshing fruit we know and love today. Still packed with loads of flavor, watermelon has become a taste associated with summer in modern Greece, with many tavernas offering their own takes on the classic watermelon margarita.

Serve with alcohol for a sweet summer cocktail, or skip the booze for a refreshing mocktail.

¼ cup (60 g) kosher salt or coarse
　　sea salt
2 teaspoons granulated sugar
1 teaspoon lime zest
3 lb (1.4 kg) watermelon

FOR ONE MARGARITA
1 lime wedge
1½ fl oz (45 ml) tequila blanco
1 fl oz (30 ml) lime juice
1 fl oz (30 ml) Cointreau
⅓ cup (75 ml) watermelon juice

TIP: *Add ice to the glasses and not directly to the pitcher, as the ice will dilute the margaritas.*

1. Combine the salt, sugar, and lime zest in a small bowl. Rub together to work the zest into the salt and sugar, which will release the essential oils and help intensify the lime flavor. Set aside.

2. Remove and discard the watermelon rind. Coarsely chop the fruit, then add the pieces to a blender. Process until smooth. Pour the watermelon puree through a fine sieve set over a large bowl or pitcher. Discard the solids, reserving the juice.

3. To make a single margarita: Rub the lime wedge around the rim of a margarita glass. Dip the top of the glass in the salt mixture to coat the rim. Add ice to the glass and pour in the tequila, lime juice, and Cointreau. Finally, pour in the watermelon juice and gently stir.

4. For a pitcher of margaritas: In a large pitcher, combine the tequila, lime juice, Cointreau, and 2 cups (450 ml) watermelon juice, stirring well. Rub the lime wedge around the rims of 6 margarita glasses, then dip the top of each glass in the salt mixture to coat the rim. Fill with ice and divide the mixture in the pitcher among the glasses.

FALL

A *Celebration* OF *Demeter*

Fall is the season of Demeter, goddess of the harvest. It is a season of completion and endings, of preparing for the future and new beginnings. Mythologically, fall is when Demeter grieves the return of her daughter, Persephone, to the Underworld.

We can see that grief play out in *Lore Olympus*, and Demeter is often overbearing as a result. She is closed off and unyielding, unwilling to listen to Persephone's complaints or needs. And though Demeter can come off as harsh, her love for her daughter is never in question.

Historically, autumn was the season when the ancient Greeks celebrated Demeter, giving thanks for their harvests and looking forward to the next year's crops. Demeter was celebrated as the "Bringer of Wealth," though in this instance the wealth they meant was the bounty of the earth, not the financial version associated with Hades. She was also celebrated as the goddess of "carrying of things laid down," meaning it was a time to lay down their tools of the fields, giving them over instead to Demeter for a few months while they let the land rest.

As the cold nights grew longer, the storms more unpredictable, and the seas more dangerous, people drew closer together to ensure their survival through the coming winter. And as their focus shifted from the harvest to the home, there was a special festival thrown to celebrate women and their role in the community. This festival was called the Thesmophoria, and it was a women-only festival that was held every fall to celebrate Demeter and Persephone; it was viewed as a way to renew the land and the fertility of those who participated.

The rituals at the Thesmophoria took place over three days. On the first day, women would ascend to the shrine to prepare animal sacrifices and to set up the tents they would live in during the festival. On the second day, they would fast and mourn as a way to reenact Demeter's sorrow while Persephone was

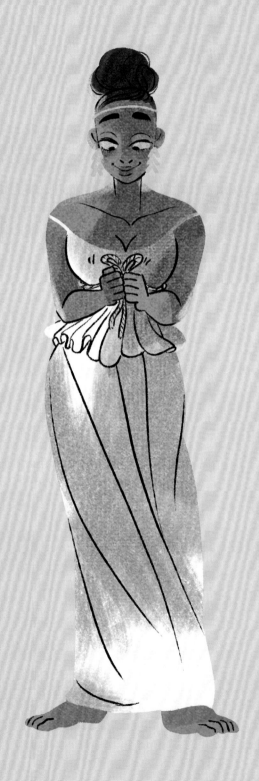

away in the Underworld. On the third day, women would pray to the goddess of childbirth, hoping to have a child in the upcoming year. Scholars are unsure of what other rituals happened during the festival—though they probably included lots of wine and feasting. What we do know is that the Thesmophoria was a time of women coming together and celebrating their community.

In *Lore Olympus*, we see the mortal realm through the eyes of Persephone, Demeter, and the nymphs who reside there. These women all toil together tirelessly to ensure that humanity is able to thrive, creating a strong community that works together to provide for their families and achieve success professionally (the Barley Mother brand is worth billions!). Their depiction in *Lore Olympus* very much reflects what the ancient world would have looked like for rural women. They would have worked together sowing, planting, and gathering the harvests. They would have provided for their families and cared for the young. And they would have come together to celebrate their community.

Celebrate the bountiful harvest with these recipes, designed for embracing the flavors of autumn. And make sure you give thanks to Demeter, Persephone, and the hardworking nymphs!

Pasta Flora

Serves — 8   *Prep time* — 35 minutes   *Cook time* — 50 to 60 minutes   *Extra time* — 1 hour, chilling

Hestia, goddess of the home, is usually a comforting and soothing presence in *Lore Olympus*. And much like the goddess, this simple but sumptuous dessert is one that will fill you with warmth and joy.

Pasta flora is the Greek take on the Italian dessert pasta frolla, or fruit pastry. This jam tart is a delicious autumn treat that can be made with any flavor of preserves—strawberry, raspberry, orange, pomegranate, plum, apple, or whatever your heart desires. You can even change it up every time you make it!

9 oz (250 g) unsalted butter, softened

⅓ cup (65 g) granulated sugar

1 egg yolk

2 tablespoons brandy

1 teaspoon lemon zest

1 teaspoon vanilla extract

2¾ cups (345 g) all-purpose flour

1 teaspoon baking powder

1 pinch salt

1 cup (320 g) fruit jam or preserves

1. Using the paddle attachment of a stand mixer, beat the butter on high speed until light and fluffy, about 5 minutes. Gradually add the sugar, egg yolk, brandy, lemon zest, and vanilla, beating until combined.

2. Combine the flour, baking powder, and salt in a bowl. With the mixer on slow speed, gradually add the flour mixture to the butter mixture, mixing until just combined. Remove the dough from the mixing bowl and gather into a ball. Break off roughly a quarter of the dough and shape into a log. Shape the larger piece into a round disc, about 1½ inches (4 cm) thick. Place both pieces on a plate, cover with plastic wrap, and chill in the refrigerator for 1 hour.

3. Preheat the oven to 350 degrees F (180 degrees C).

4. Lay a sheet of waxed paper or parchment paper on a work surface, placing the disc of dough in the center. Lay another sheet of paper on top. Use a rolling pin to roll into a circle 11 inches (28 cm) in diameter. Remove the top sheet of paper and use the bottom sheet to invert the dough into a 9-inch (23 cm) round springform cake pan or loose-bottomed tart pan. Remove the paper and press the dough to the edges of the pan and about 1 inch (2.5 cm) up the sides.

TIP: *Don't worry if the dough breaks! When cold it can easily crumble, but as it warms up it is easy to mold and press into place.*

5. Pour the jam over the prepared base and spread evenly to the sides. Cut the remaining portion of dough into eight pieces roughly equal in size. Roll each out into a long snake and place the strips over the jam, creating a lattice pattern.

6. Bake in the preheated oven until the crust is golden brown and pulling away from the sides of the pan, 50 to 60 minutes. Let cool to room temperature so that the jam sets before removing the rim of the pan, slicing, and serving.

Artemis's Crepes

Serves — **4**   *Yield* — **8 crepes**   *Prep time* — **30 minutes**   *Cook time* — **25 minutes**

Move over, Poseidon's kitty-shaped pancakes! Retsina, Artemis's cat, is spoiled rotten and now enjoys only the finer things in life—so only a thin, rich, buttery crepe will suffice. Artemis has perfected just a few items in the kitchen, but this is her crowning jewel for her beloved pet.

Though this delicious crepe recipe is not for mortal kittens, it *is* a brilliant way to upgrade your brunch menu or cook a fast and easy dinner on a weeknight. If you have a sweet tooth, garnish with fresh strawberries, blackberries, blueberries, Nutella, or pomegranate compote. If you prefer your crepes savory, try adding ham and cheese to make a delightful anytime dish.

FOR THE CREPES

1 cup (125 g) all-purpose flour

2 eggs

½ cup (120 ml) whole milk

2 tablespoons (30 g) butter, melted

¼ teaspoon salt

3 tablespoons (45 g) butter, softened, for greasing the pan

FOR THE GARNISH

1 orange

½ cup (90 g) pomegranate arils

FOR THE CHOCOLATE TAHINI SAUCE

½ cup (75 g) dark chocolate chips

3 tablespoons extra-virgin olive oil

¼ cup (80 g) honey

¼ cup (60 g) tahini

½ teaspoon vanilla extract

1 pinch salt

1. Make the crepe batter: Place the flour, eggs, milk, melted butter, and salt in a blender. Process in short bursts just until the mixture is homogeneous and smooth. (If you don't have a blender, whisk everything together in a mixing bowl.) Set aside.

2. Prepare the garnish: Use a sharp paring knife to slice off both ends of the orange. Stand the orange on a cutting board and cut off the peel and white pith from top to bottom. Slice into thin rounds and set aside.

3. Make the sauce: Add enough water to a medium saucepan to cover the bottom by 1 inch (2.5 cm). Place over medium heat. Place the chocolate chips, olive oil, and honey in a large heatproof bowl. Once the water in the saucepan is just starting to simmer, place the bowl over the pan and reduce the heat to low. Stir the ingredients gently with a spatula until the chocolate is melted and the sauce is

MEOW!

MEOW!

MEOW!

CONTINUED

Retsina is an ancient Greek wine that has been made for over two thousand years. The process relies heavily on pine resin, which lines the barrels in which the wine is aged and gives it a faint pine taste. Light and fruity, this white wine is often made locally in different villages and towns in modern Greece.

smooth, 1 to 2 minutes. Remove the pan from the heat and transfer the bowl to a work surface, placing a towel underneath it. Stir in the tahini, vanilla, and salt until smooth. Set aside.

4. Make the crepes: Lightly grease an 8-inch (20 cm) frying pan with some of the softened butter and place over medium heat. Flick some water from the tap onto the pan; if it immediately sizzles, it's ready.

5. Pour approximately ¼ cup (60 ml) crepe batter into the pan. Quickly tilt the pan in a circular motion, allowing the batter to spread to the sides and creating a thin layer covering the entire bottom of the pan. Cook until the edges look dry and bubbles begin to appear on top of the crepe, about 2 minutes. Flip and cook the other side until golden, about 1 minute more.

6. Remove the crepe to a plate and cover with aluminum foil to keep warm while you prepare more crepes with the remaining batter, greasing the pan with butter before each crepe.

7. Assemble: Drizzle a little sauce on each crepe before folding it into quarters. If the sauce was made far in advance and has cooled and thickened, reheat in the microwave until warmed through, 20 to 30 seconds, before drizzling. Top with additional sauce and garnish with orange slices and pomegranate arils.

Mulled Pomegranate Juice

Serves — 4   *Prep time* — 5 minutes   *Cook time* — 15 minutes

When the nights start to draw in and the crisp fall evenings arrive, there is nothing nicer than a cup of hot mulled pomegranate juice. The aromatic spices, including cinnamon and allspice, make this a rich and full-bodied take on traditional mulled drinks like cider.

Pomegranates, like apples, ripen in the autumn. And in ancient times, they were thought by some to be a type of apple; the Latin word for the fruit literally means "seeded apple," and in Ireland they were called "wine-apples," presumably because of their rich red color.

In *Lore Olympus*, pomegranates are the fruit of the Underworld. When the ancient primordial god Tartarus takes form, he does so as a pomegranate tree— one that has only twice borne fruit. Each time, that fruit has crowned a new ruler of the Underworld: first King Hades and then Queen Persephone.

---

4 cups (1 L) pomegranate juice
   (see note)
8 allspice berries
4 star anise pods
2 cinnamon sticks
2 bay leaves
2 tablespoons honey, or to taste
   (optional)

COOK'S NOTE: *Use half pomegranate juice and half white wine for a low-ABV twist on mulled wine.*

1. Place the pomegranate juice, allspice berries, star anise pods, cinnamon sticks, and bay leaves in a small saucepan. Cover and place over medium-high heat. Bring to a simmer, then immediately reduce the heat to low. Cook gently, covered, for 15 to 20 minutes to let the spices infuse the juice. Avoid letting the mixture boil.

2. Taste and add more honey, if desired. Carefully pour the hot mulled juice through a strainer; discard the spices. Ladle into mugs and serve.

Do I look like a scoundrel to you?
I'd say 30 percent scoundrel at least.

Scoundrel Martini

Serves — 1 *Prep time* — 5 minutes

The beleaguered King of the Underworld, Hades, loves his coffee almost as much as he loves a good cocktail. Whether he's staying up all night to ensure that a certain pink goddess finds her way home safely or dealing with one of Zeus's many, many, *many* interpersonal dramas, Hades always finds a way to keep himself caffeinated and calm.

This delicious cold brew cocktail is inspired by all the best aspects of the Underworld: the crisp cold days, the earthy and bitter bite of coffee, and just a hint of our beloved scoundrel Hades's favorite liqueur. Impress your java-loving friends at a party with this caffeine-laden cocktail, or enjoy the alcohol-free version on a cold winter's evening while organizing your upcoming work week at Underworld Corp.

2 fl oz (60 ml) vodka

1 fl oz (30 ml) cold brew concentrate

½ fl oz (15 ml) coffee liqueur

¼ fl oz (7 ml) simple syrup (see tip)

3 coffee beans, for garnish

COOK'S NOTE: *If you don't have cold brew concentrate, you can use the same amount of freshly brewed espresso.*

1. Fill a cocktail shaker with ice, then fill a martini glass with ice.

2. Add the vodka, cold brew concentrate, coffee liqueur, and simple syrup to the cocktail shaker. Cover and shake vigorously until the outside of the shaker is frosty, 20 to 30 seconds.

3. Discard the ice in the martini glass. Strain the liquid from the shaker into the glass. Carefully place the coffee beans in the center of the foam.

TIP: *Simple syrup can be bought at any liquor store, but you can also easily make your own. Combine 1 part sugar and 1 part water in a small saucepan over medium-high heat. Bring to a boil and stir just until the sugar is dissolved. Allow to cool, then store any extra in the refrigerator for up to 1 month.*

Hera's Moussaka

Serves — 4 to 6   *Prep time* — 1 hour   *Cook time* — 45 minutes
Extra time — 15 minutes, resting

There are only a few family dinner moments in the comic, the most awkward of which features Olympus's worst dinner party: Zeus, Hera, Hebe, Hades, and—invited at the very last minute—Persephone. It is a strained affair, with Persephone underdressed and unprepared to run into her crush, and Zeus and Hera deliberately picking a fight with each other for the entire meal. At least their spat allows Hades and Persephone to slip away into the rose garden to shamelessly flirt, so it's not *all* terrible.

Hera and Zeus might not have a conventional marriage, but they do occasionally find moments of peace to sit down to dinner together. And when they do, they serve the ultimate family-style comfort food: moussaka. While it wasn't popularized in the mortal realm until the 1920s by Nikolaos Tselementes, one of Greece's most influential chefs, the king and queen of the gods have been dining on this dish for millennia—and this is Hera's take on the rich combination of eggplant, ground meat, tomato sauce, and cheese.

---

1 large eggplant, cut into ¼-inch (6 mm) slices

2 teaspoons salt

2 large yellow or gold potatoes, peeled and cut into ¼-inch (6 mm) slices

¼ cup (60 ml) extra-virgin olive oil, divided

½ cup (60 g) freshly grated Parmesan or Kefalotiri cheese

1. Sprinkle the eggplant slices with the salt and place in a colander set in the sink or on a plate. Let the eggplant rest until all the bitter juices have drained, 30 to 60 minutes.

2. Meanwhile, make the meat sauce: Heat the olive oil in a large sauté pan over medium-high heat. Add the ground beef and pork. Cook and stir until evenly browned, about 5 minutes. Add the onion and cook until softened, 2 to 3 minutes. Stir in the tomato paste and cook briefly before adding the strained tomatoes, allspice, cinnamon, sugar, and salt and pepper. Bring to a simmer and cook, partially covered, until the mixture has thickened and all the excess liquid has evaporated, 15 to 20 minutes.

3. Preheat the oven to 400 degrees F (200 degrees C). Line two baking sheets with parchment paper.

4. Once the juices have drained from the eggplant, rinse the slices and pat dry with paper towels.

CONTINUED

FOR THE MEAT SAUCE

3 tablespoons extra-virgin olive oil

8 oz (225 g) ground beef

8 oz (225 g) ground pork

½ small red onion, grated on the
    large holes of a box grater

1 tablespoon tomato paste

1 cup (250 ml) strained tomatoes
    (passata) or crushed tomatoes

5 allspice berries

½ teaspoon ground cinnamon

1 pinch sugar

salt and pepper, to taste

FOR THE BÉCHAMEL

3 tablespoons extra-virgin olive oil

3 tablespoons all-purpose flour

2 cups (475 ml) whole milk

2 egg yolks, beaten

salt, to taste

5. Brush the eggplant and potato slices on both sides with 1 tablespoon olive oil, then lay in a single layer on the prepared baking sheets.

6. Bake in the preheated oven, turning once, until both the eggplant and potatoes are tender and the potatoes are golden brown, about 20 minutes. Remove from the oven and let cool slightly.

7. Grease an 8-to-9-inch (20 to 23 cm) square baking dish with olive oil. Reduce the oven temperature to 50 degrees F (180 degrees C).

8. Make the béchamel: Place the olive oil and flour in a medium saucepan over medium heat. Cook until the flour starts to take on a golden brown color and smells nutty. Reduce the heat to low and gradually pour in the milk, whisking constantly. Cook until thickened (the sauce should coat the back of a spoon without sliding off). Remove from the heat and whisk in the beaten egg yolks. Season with salt and set aside.

9. Assemble the moussaka: Place the potatoes in the prepared pan in a single layer, followed by the eggplant. Top with the meat sauce. Carefully pour the béchamel over the top. Sprinkle with the grated cheese.

10. Bake in the preheated oven until bubbly and the top is a deep golden brown, 45 to 55 minutes. Remove from the oven and let rest for 10 to 15 minutes before slicing and serving.

TIP: *You can make either the meat sauce or the béchamel (or both) ahead of time and assemble the next day. If you're feeding a larger crowd, you can double this recipe and use a 9-by-13-inch (22 by 33 cm) baking dish.*

Rapini, Sausage, and Feta Pasta

Serves — 4   *Prep time* — 10 minutes   *Cook time* — 15 minutes

Nothing screams big and bold quite like the god of war, Ares. Ares is larger than life, his presence literally causes conflict, and he's unabashedly proud of who he is—over-the-top, crass, silly, and a little kinky (sugar cubes, anyone?).

As much as Ares acts like he's got the "biggest_dickest"—to quote the handle he chose for Zeus's virtual meeting of the Olympians—he really has a huge heart. He's protective of the people he loves, adores his family, and always has time for Storge and his hamster—even if he does like to stir up trouble, just because. (He is the child of Hera and Zeus, after all; he loves drama.)

This dish is similarly bold, and packed with heat and spice—just like a certain orange and yellow god.

---

12 oz (340 g) pasta, such as fettuccine or penne

2 tablespoons extra-virgin olive oil, plus extra for serving

8 oz (225 g) spicy Italian sausage (or Greek loukaniko), sliced

2 garlic cloves, thinly sliced

8 oz (225 g) chopped rapini (or broccolini)

7 oz (200 g) sheep's-milk feta cheese, crumbled

½ cup (120 ml) lemon juice

crushed red chile pepper flakes or Aleppo pepper flakes, to taste (optional)

1. Bring a large pot of salted water to a boil. Add the pasta and cook according to the package directions. Drain well, but do not rinse. Return to the pot and set aside.

2. Heat the olive oil in a large frying pan over medium-high heat. Add the sausage and cook until evenly browned, about 5 minutes. Add the garlic and then the rapini. Cook, stirring, until the rapini is wilted, 6 to 8 minutes.

3. Add the crumbled feta to the pan and stir until partially melted. Add the lemon juice and pasta, and use a pair of tongs to toss to coat the pasta evenly in the sauce. Sprinkle with crushed red chile pepper, if desired, then remove from the heat and serve immediately with a drizzle of olive oil over each serving.

Aphrodite's Roasted Beet and Pear Soup with Yogurt Crema

Serves — 6   *Prep time* — 15 minutes   *Cook time* — 15 minutes

When the temperature drops, there is nothing better than soup with crusty bread. This rich beet-and-pear soup is a stunning blend of sweet and savory—and, according to Aphrodite, it might be the latest addition to your beauty routine.

The ancient Greeks believed that eating beet soup could make you more attractive, since it was said that Aphrodite ate beets to enhance her beauty. Beets were also painted all over the walls of brothels in Pompeii, as the root vegetable was considered an aphrodisiac by the ancient Greeks and Romans. In short, beets have long been considered the vegetable of love and desire.

It's hard not to fall for this soup; it's healthy, simple to make, and a staple of the goddess of love and beauty.

FOR THE CREMA

½ cup (120 g) plain Greek yogurt (2 to 5%)

7 oz (200 g) sheep's-milk feta cheese, crumbled

1 tablespoon lemon juice, plus more to taste

FOR THE SOUP

1 lb (450 g) beets, peeled and cut into chunks

1 large pear, such as Anjou, peeled, cored, and sliced

1 carrot, peeled and sliced

½ onion, roughly chopped

3½ cups (825 ml) vegetable stock

¼ cup (60 ml) extra-virgin olive oil

salt, to taste

chopped fresh dill, for garnish

1. Make the crema: Combine the yogurt, feta, and lemon juice in a blender or food processor. Puree until smooth. Add a little more lemon juice to taste, if desired. Set aside. You can also prepare the crema up to 1 day in advance and store in the fridge until needed.

2. Make the soup: Combine the beets, pear, carrot, onion, and vegetable stock in a large pot. Cover and place over medium-high heat. Bring to a boil, then reduce the heat and simmer until all the vegetables are soft, 15 to 20 minutes. Remove from the heat.

3. Using an immersion blender, carefully puree the vegetables in the pot until smooth. With the blender running, slowly drizzle in the olive oil in a thin, steady stream; this emulsifies the oil and creates a creamy texture to the soup. Taste and season with salt. Return to medium heat to heat through.

4. Ladle the soup into serving bowls and garnish with a drizzle of the crema and a sprinkling of fresh dill.

Sesame-Crusted Feta with Pomegranate Honey Syrup

Serves — 4   *Prep time* — 10 minutes   *Cook time* — 25 minutes

Move over, ambrosia—feta is truly the food of the gods. And this sweet, crunchy, salty, tart, and sharp dish is one that will have all your senses singing hymns to the Olympians. Traditionally this dish is drizzled with honey, but swapping out honey for pomegranate syrup makes this a romantic and swoon-worthy fall dish.

References to feta appear in Homer's *The Odyssey*, written in the eighth century B.C.E. It is the story of Odysseus's journey home after the Trojan War (the one that began with a golden apple). Odysseus makes a cameo in *Lore Olympus* when he sneaks into Zeus's party and immediately comes under fire from Poseidon, the sea god being one of the main antagonists preventing Odysseus from returning home in the myth.

Zeus, did you invite *Odysseus!?*

FOR THE POMEGRANATE HONEY SYRUP

1 cup (225 ml) pomegranate juice
3 tablespoons honey

FOR THE FETA

1 block (8 oz / 225 g) sheep's-milk
   feta cheese
1 egg, beaten
½ cup (60 g) all-purpose flour
½ cup (75 g) sesame seeds
pepper, to taste
¼ cup (60 ml) extra-virgin
   olive oil

1. Make the pomegranate honey syrup: Place the pomegranate juice in a small heavy saucepan over medium heat. Bring to a boil and cook, uncovered and without stirring, until reduced by more than half to approximately 3 to 4 tablespoons, 15 to 18 minutes. To prevent burning, start checking at the 10-to-12-minute mark to make sure that the juice is not reducing too quickly. Remove from the heat.

2. Add the honey to the reduced pomegranate juice and stir until well combined. Set aside. You can make the pomegranate honey syrup up to 1 week in advance; just let cool to room temperature and store in an airtight container in the refrigerator until needed.

3. Prepare the feta: Slice the feta into four "fingers" and place in the freezer to help the cheese hold its shape while you prepare the other ingredients.

CONTINUED

4. Set out the egg, flour, and sesame seeds in three separate shallow dishes. Season the egg and the flour with pepper.

5. Remove the feta from the freezer and dredge each finger first in egg, then in flour, and then in egg again before finishing with sesame seeds. Evenly coat all sides.

6. Pour the oil into an 8-inch (20 cm) frying pan to a depth of about ½ inch. Heat over medium heat. Add the feta fingers and cook until golden brown, about 2 minutes per side. Remove the fingers to paper towels to absorb any excess oil.

7. Place the feta fingers on a serving plate and drizzle with pomegranate honey syrup to taste. Enjoy immediately while hot, as the feta will harden as it cools.

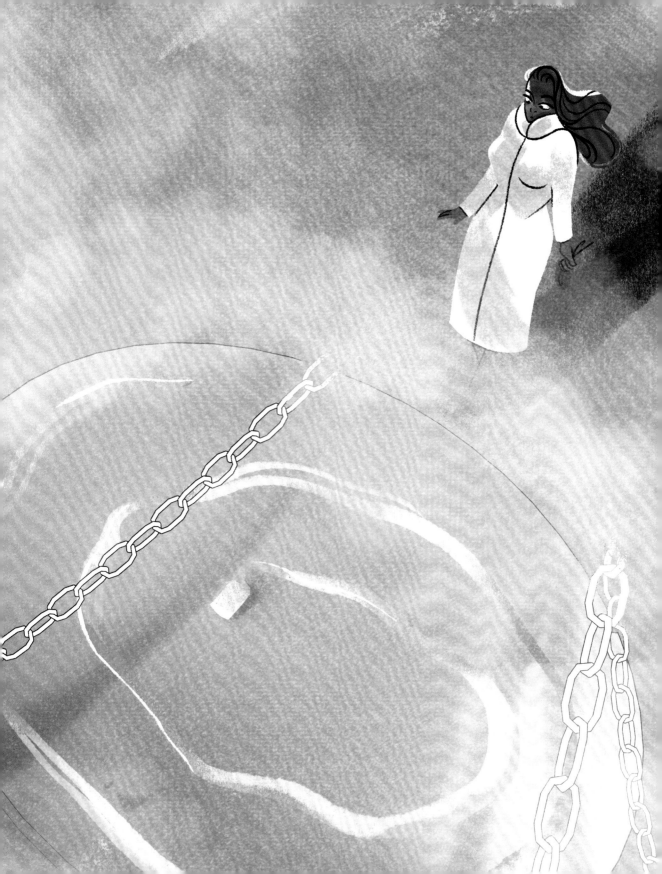

Red Wine Pomegranate Poached Pears

Serves — 6   *Prep time* — 20 minutes   *Cook time* — 40 minutes

Reminiscent of baby Dionysus setting off on his first quest (to help his adoptive mother, Persephone, battle a Titan), these pears are a journey for the senses. Rich red wine, roasted ripe pears, decadent pomegranate—an absolute feast for the senses, born out of a collaboration between the god of wine and the Queen of the Underworld. A true gift of the gods.

The ancient Greeks believed that all fruit was a gift from the gods, but pears were special. They were associated with the goddess Hera and believed to be symbols of fertility. And while they're not as prominent as golden apples or pomegranates in mythology, their praises were sung by Homer, the blind poet, in his epic poem *The Odyssey*.

FOR THE POACHED PEARS

2 cups (475 ml) red wine

1 cup (240 ml) pomegranate juice

1 cup (200 g) granulated sugar

3 strips orange peel

5 whole cloves

5 black peppercorns

1 teaspoon vanilla bean paste or vanilla extract

6 firm medium-sized pears, such as Bartlett or Anjou (see tip)

½ cup (65 g) shelled pistachios

1. Make the poached pears: Place the wine, pomegranate juice, sugar, orange peel, cloves, peppercorns, and vanilla in a medium saucepan. Cover and bring to a boil. Reduce the heat to a simmer and cook until the sugar is dissolved, 3 to 5 minutes.

2. Meanwhile, carefully peel the pears using a vegetable peeler or paring knife. Leave the pears whole with the stem intact.

3. Gently place the pears in the red wine mixture. Cover and simmer gently over medium-low heat, turning occasionally, until the pears are soft, about 15 minutes.

4. Remove from the heat and let the pears cool in the pan for at least 15 minutes, then remove with a slotted spoon. Set aside.

5. Place the pan with the red wine mixture over medium-high heat. Bring to a boil and cook, uncovered, until thickened and reduced by more than half, 10 to 15 minutes. Remove from the heat and let cool completely.

CONTINUED

FOR THE MASCARPONE CREAM

½ cup (120 ml) heavy whipping cream, chilled

¼ cup (30 g) powdered sugar

½ cup (120 g) mascarpone cheese, at room temperature (see note)

¼ teaspoon vanilla bean paste or vanilla extract

COOK'S NOTE: *To make this a vegan dessert, serve with a coconut-based vanilla ice cream instead of the mascarpone cream.*

6. Place the pistachios in a small frying pan over medium heat. Toast, stirring occasionally, until fragrant and lightly browned, about 10 minutes. Remove to a cutting board and chop when cool to the touch.

7. Make the mascarpone cream: Place the whipped cream and powdered sugar in a mixing bowl and beat to stiff peaks. Add the mascarpone and vanilla, then beat briefly to combine.

8. To serve: Place each pear in a shallow bowl. Add a heaping tablespoonful of the cream next to it. Drizzle with the cooled syrup, then sprinkle with pistachios.

TIP: *You can get the pears to stand upright for a pretty presentation by cutting off a small portion of the bottom so that they have a flat surface to rest on.*

Pomegranates

Pomegranates grow wild all over Greece and fruit in the late summer/early autumn. You can find them in cities, in orchards, and in the ruins of ancient sites. Hauntingly, these fruits grow among the tombs and graves of the ancient graveyard at Kerameikos, where the procession to Eleusis would begin each spring and fall to celebrate Persephone's descent to and return from the Underworld.

Persephone's Baklava

Serves — 6   *Prep time* — 25 minutes   *Cook time* — 35 minutes   *Extra time* — 2 hours, resting

We get to see how delicious Persephone's super-secret baklava recipe is in Episode 52, "Going Down," when she tries to give Hades some of the homemade treat as a thank-you gift for his help and support. And though he initially declines, he is ultimately unable to resist the delectable dessert.

Baklava, with its rich honey, flaky pastry, and hint of springtime herbs, is a time-honored dish in Greece, and Persephone has been perfecting her version for years. She based it on a recipe invented by Hestia, the goddess of home and hearth, but with a few alterations so that it's infused with its own kind of magic—able to mend a broken heart, please a crowd, or impress a hunky Underworld god.

Just don't tell Hestia that Persephone changed the original recipe. You know how she gets about these things.

FOR THE SYRUP

1 cup water
¾ cup (150 g) granulated sugar
3 strips lemon peel
1 cinnamon stick
butter, for greasing the pie dish

FOR THE BAKLAVA

1½ cups (150 g) walnut halves
¼ cup (50 g) plus 1 tablespoon
    granulated sugar, divided
1 teaspoon ground cinnamon
¼ teaspoon ground cloves
½ (1 lb / 450 g) package phyllo
    pastry (7 to 8 sheets)
5 tablespoons unsalted butter,
    melted
½ cup (120 ml) whole milk
1 egg

1. Make the syrup: In a small saucepan, combine the water, sugar, lemon peel, and cinnamon stick and place over medium heat. Bring to a boil and cook until the sugar is fully dissolved, 1 to 2 minutes. Remove from the heat and let cool completely.

2. Make the baklava: Preheat the oven to 350 degrees F (180 degrees C). Grease a 9-inch (23 cm) round pie dish.

3. Place the walnuts, 1 tablespoon sugar, cinnamon, and cloves in a food processor. Process in several short bursts until the mixture looks like coarse sand.

4. Lay out a sheet of phyllo pastry with a short end facing you and lightly brush with the melted butter. Evenly scatter 1 to 2 tablespoons of the walnut mixture over the sheet. Working with the short end closest to you, start gathering up the sheet accordion-style until you reach the other end. Curl the phyllo into a spiral and place in the center of the pie dish. Repeat with the remaining phyllo sheets and nut mixture, laying each phyllo accordion next to the previous one until you've reached the edge of the pie dish. Scatter any remaining nut mixture over the top.

5. Whisk together the milk, egg, and ¼ cup sugar until well combined. Pour slowly and evenly over the phyllo.

6. Bake in the preheated oven until the top is a deep golden brown, 35 to 40 minutes.

7. Remove from the oven and immediately pour the cooled syrup over the baklava, ladling it bit by bit and letting it gradually soak into the pastry. Let rest until the syrup has soaked in fully, about 2 hours.

TIP: *Don't cover the baklava at any point before serving, as this will make the phyllo soggy. Store it uncovered in a cool oven or a container. Leftovers will keep for 2 to 3 days at room temperature.*

CELEBRATE
AT THE

Fall
HARVEST
FESTIVAL
Feast

*Roasted Fall
Vegetables
with Halloumi*
pg 149

Zucchini
Rice Bake
pg 155

Apple Olive
Oil Cake
pg 158

Zeus's
Golden
Appletini
pg 157

Warm Honey-
Roasted Carrot
and Pearl
Couscous Salad
pg 150

It is time for one last celebration before fall officially fades into winter: the Harvest Festival!

Much like the party that Demeter would throw for her hardworking nymphs at the turn of the season, this feast revels in the flavors of fall and highlights the many wonderful fruits and vegetables of the goddess of the harvest. Roast all of your favorite fall veggies to perfection—and don't forget to top with a healthy serving of halloumi—or cozy up to a warm honey-roasted carrot and pearl couscous salad. Channel your inner Hestia to bake a delightfully aromatic apple cake, or sing the praises of apples in a different way with a delightful cinnamon twist on an appletini.

However you choose to host your own Harvest Festival, just make sure to do it in style—and with a Demeter-approved amount of produce!

Roasted Fall Vegetables with Halloumi

Serves — 4   *Prep time* — 10 minutes   *Cook time* — 15 minutes

The nymphs of the mortal realm work around the clock with Demeter and Persephone to protect nature and the harvest—but that doesn't mean they don't know how to party! And they know that the secret to a perfect evening of dancing under the stars is to have a hearty meal beforehand, and preferably not be trapped doing a ton of dishes afterward.

Enter this sheet pan bake that is simple, filling, and absolutely delicious—and with only one pan needed to cook, it's ideal for easy cleanup. Roasted root vegetables and salty halloumi make for a warming autumn dish that can act either as a main when paired with rice or couscous, or solo as a standout side dish. Serve with wine, crusty bread, and a side of all the best gossip in the mortal realm.

¼ cup (60 ml) extra-virgin olive oil

¼ teaspoon dried Greek oregano

¼ teaspoon dried thyme

¼ teaspoon salt, or to taste

pepper, to taste

8 oz (225 g) sweet potato, peeled

8 oz (225 g) purple sweet potato, peeled

1 large carrot (approximately 5 oz / 150 g)

6 shallots (approximately 5 oz / 150 g), peeled and left whole

1 block (8 oz / 225 g) halloumi, cut into 8 slices

1. Preheat the oven to 425 degrees F (220 degrees C). Line a sheet pan with parchment paper.

2. Combine the olive oil, oregano, thyme, salt, and pepper in a large mixing bowl and stir.

3. Cut the sweet potatoes into 1-inch (2.5 cm) chunks. The carrots take longer to cook, so slice them crosswise into slightly smaller pieces, about ¾ inch (2 cm). Add the sweet potatoes, carrots, and shallots to the oil mixture and toss to coat, then transfer to the prepared sheet pan, leaving the remaining oil in the bowl.

4. Gently add the halloumi to the bowl and turn to coat in the oil. Place on the sheet pan, spreading out the vegetables and halloumi in an even single layer.

5. Bake in the preheated oven until the halloumi is golden on the bottom and the vegetables are tender, 15 to 20 minutes. Serve immediately.

Warm Honey-Roasted Carrot and Pearl Couscous Salad

Serves — 4   *Prep time* — 15 minutes   *Cook time* — 30 minutes

Thanatos, the god of death, goes through quite a transformation throughout *Lore Olympus*. He first appears in the story as an entitled, lazy god who is hooking up with his boss's girlfriend. He's fallen into a lot of toxic habits and relationships, and is generally stuck in a rut.

However, the magic of a fleeing nymph and a pretzel by moonlight turn him from snarky boy to sweet boyfriend. Thanatos throws himself into learning about who he is, what he wants, and how to be a better god. His relationship with Daphne is a sweet reversal of the one he had with Minthe (where she literally hid him in closets and refused to acknowledge his existence).

Thanatos starts to take care of himself and his diet. He leans into the health-conscious lifestyle that Daphne lives and even makes her healthy snacks for her visit to the mortal realm. This delicious honey-roasted carrot and pearl couscous salad is exactly the kind of meal Thanatos would prepare for Daphne—filled with nutrients, bright colors, and love.

---

2 lb (900 g) carrots, halved and cut into sticks

2 tablespoons plus 2 teaspoons extra-virgin olive oil, divided

4 tablespoons honey, divided

¼ teaspoon salt

1 tablespoon fresh thyme leaves or 1 teaspoon dried

pepper, to taste

1 cup (160 g) pearl couscous

1½ cups (350 ml) vegetable broth

2 tablespoons chopped fresh flat-leaf parsley

1 cup (135 g) hazelnuts, roughly chopped

4 oz (110 g) sheep's-milk feta cheese, crumbled

1. Preheat the oven to 400 degrees F (200 degrees C) and line a baking sheet with parchment paper.

2. Toss the carrots with 2 tablespoons olive oil, 2 tablespoons honey, the salt, thyme, and pepper. Spread in an even layer on the baking sheet.

3. Roast the carrots in the preheated oven until tender and caramelized, 25 to 30 minutes.

4. Meanwhile, in a medium saucepan, heat 2 teaspoons olive oil over medium-high heat. Add the couscous and cook, stirring, until lightly toasted, 2 to 3 minutes. Add the vegetable broth and bring to a boil. Cover, reduce the heat to medium low, and cook until all the liquid is absorbed and the couscous is tender, 12 to 14 minutes. Remove from the heat and stir in the parsley.

CONTINUED

5. While the couscous and carrots are cooking, place the hazelnuts in a medium frying pan over medium heat. Toast, stirring occasionally, until lightly browned and fragrant, 5 to 10 minutes.

6. Assemble the salad: On a large serving platter, spread out the couscous, then top with the carrots. Crumble the feta over the top, scatter with the toasted hazelnuts, and drizzle with 2 tablespoons honey. Enjoy warm.

Zucchini Rice Bake

Serves — 6   *Prep time* — 15 minutes   *Cook time* — 35 minutes

Both ancient and modern Greeks organized their diets around the seasons, retiring recipes when their ingredients weren't at peak freshness. The seasons have long been important in mythology, and one key figure in the stories of the seasons is Metis, the Titaness of wisdom.

Metis is the mother of Demeter, Hera, and Hestia. She raises all of her daughters to be soldiers in the upcoming war against Kronos, determined that the season of the power-hungry Titan of time will come to an end and that her daughters will help create a world free of tyranny. And like many other fertility goddesses before her, she gives her life in order to build a better world for her children.

Her daughters honor and remember her in the harvest of fresh vegetables, in cooking by the fireside, and in sharing stories. This dish draws on that tradition, using fresh zucchini—baked with love and a lot of cheese—to create a scrumptious vegetarian dish meant to be shared with friends and family.

---

3 tablespoons extra-virgin olive oil

4 green onions, chopped

3 cups (450 g) grated zucchini (2 to 3 medium zucchini)

1½ cups (285 g) medium-grain rice, such as Calrose

3¼ cups (750 ml) hot water

1½ cups (175 g) shredded Manchego or Kefalograviera cheese, divided

salt and pepper, to taste

3 tablespoons chopped fresh mint

3 tablespoons chopped fresh parsley

lemon wedges, for serving

1. In a large ovenproof sauté pan or Dutch oven, heat the olive oil over medium heat. Add the green onions and cook until just softened, 2 to 3 minutes. Add the zucchini and cook, stirring occasionally, until dry and just starting to take color, 8 to 10 minutes.

2. Add the rice and stir to coat in the oil, then pour in the hot water. Bring to a gentle simmer, then stir in two-thirds of the cheese and season with salt and pepper. Taste the cooking liquid at this point; it should be just a little saltier than you want the finished dish to be, as the rice will absorb some of the salt.

3. Stir in the mint and parsley, then sprinkle the remaining cheese over the top. Do not stir, so that the cheese will form a nice crust on top when baked.

4. Transfer to the preheated oven and bake until the rice is tender, about 20 minutes. Serve with the lemon wedges to sprinkle lemon juice over each portion.

Zeus's Golden Appletini

Yield — 1 appletini   *Prep time* — 10 minutes   *Cook time* — 5 minutes

Zeus is a god of distinguished tastes—or so he wants to believe. He thinks he is incredibly cool and well respected, and everyone (except for his wife, Hera) mostly humors him in this delusion. The pompous king's signature drink is an appletini, and while there are a lot of reasons to dislike Zeus, his love of this delightful cocktail is not one.

Apples feature heavily in Greek mythology. Zeus famously solves the problem of the golden apple of discord by choosing a mortal to decide which goddess is the most beautiful. It goes about as well as you'd think it would and ends with the Trojan War. Classic Zeus.

An appletini is also classic, though we've put a fantastic cinnamon spin on this recipe to wow your taste buds—and your guests!

FOR THE APPLE CINNAMON SYRUP

1 cup (240 ml) apple juice
½ cup (100 g) granulated sugar
1 cinnamon stick

FOR THE APPLETINI

1½ fl oz (45 ml) vodka
½ fl oz (15 ml) Becherovka
½ fl oz (15 ml) apple juice
½ fl oz (15 ml) apple cinnamon syrup

1. Make the apple cinnamon syrup: Combine the apple juice, sugar, and cinnamon stick in a small saucepan. Bring to a boil over high heat and continue to boil until reduced by half, about 5 minutes. Remove from the heat and let cool. (See tip.)

2. Make the appletini: Fill a cocktail shaker with ice. Add the vodka, Becherovka, ½ fl oz apple juice, and apple cinnamon syrup. Cover and shake well until the outside of the shaker is frosty, 20 to 30 seconds. Remove the lid and strain into a coupe glass or martini glass.

TIP: *Any extra apple cinnamon syrup will keep in the refrigerator for up to 2 weeks.*

GOLDEN APPLES

Golden apples were sacred to the goddess Hera. According to mythology, they grew in a garden at the edge of the world and were guarded by the Hesperides. These were nymphs associated with the golden, glowing light of early evening—sometimes referred to as "Nymphs of the West" or "Daughters of the Evening." Golden apples are integral to the stories of many heroes in Greek mythology, such as the Trojan War, the myth of Atalanta, and Herakles's labors.

Apple Olive Oil Cake

Serves — 6   *Prep time* — 20 minutes   *Cook time* — 30 minutes

Have you ever wondered what fall would taste like as a dessert? This moist and light apple cake is the answer, with cinnamon, sugar, cloves, and ripe apples giving you everything you love about autumn in one bite.

Fall in Greece is considered the perfect time to visit. It's still hot, but not blisteringly so. The seas are warm. The trees and plants are full of fruit and flowers. And the summer tourists have cleared out, making the ruins and ancient sites less crowded.

The season is also traditionally sacred to Demeter, as it is when the ancient Greeks gave thanks for the abundance of their harvest, decorating her altars and temples with wheat stalks, fruit, wine, and flowers. So consider this delicious apple cake as an offering to Demeter—and enjoy the delicious blend of autumn flavors!

FOR THE CAKE

¾ cup (150 g) granulated sugar

2 large eggs

½ cup (120 ml) extra-virgin olive oil

2 cups (250 g) all-purpose flour

2 teaspoons ground cinnamon

1 teaspoon baking powder

½ teaspoon baking soda

½ teaspoon salt

¼ teaspoon ground cloves

2 cups (240 g) grated unpeeled Gala apples (grated on the large holes of a box grater)

butter or cooking spray, for greasing the pan

FOR THE TAHINI CRUMBLE

3 tablespoons tahini

3 tablespoons brown sugar, packed

¼ cup rolled oats

¼ cup all-purpose flour

1. Preheat the oven to 350 degrees F (180 degrees C). Lightly grease a 9-inch (23 cm) square cake pan.

2. Make the cake: In a medium mixing bowl, combine the granulated sugar, eggs, and olive oil and stir until combined. In a separate bowl, mix together the flour, cinnamon, baking powder, baking soda, salt, and cloves. Fold the apples into the sugar mixture, then fold in the dry ingredients, taking care not to overmix. Pour into the prepared cake pan and spread out evenly.

3. Make the tahini crumble: In a small bowl, stir together the tahini, brown sugar, oats, and flour. Mix until just combined, leaving some larger clumps of crumble. Sprinkle over the cake batter.

4. Bake in the preheated oven until a tester inserted into the center of the cake comes out clean, 30 to 35 minutes. Let cool before slicing.

COOK'S NOTE: *Though the tahini crumble takes this cake to the next level, it is optional if you're short on time.*

SEASONAL INTRODUCTION

WIN

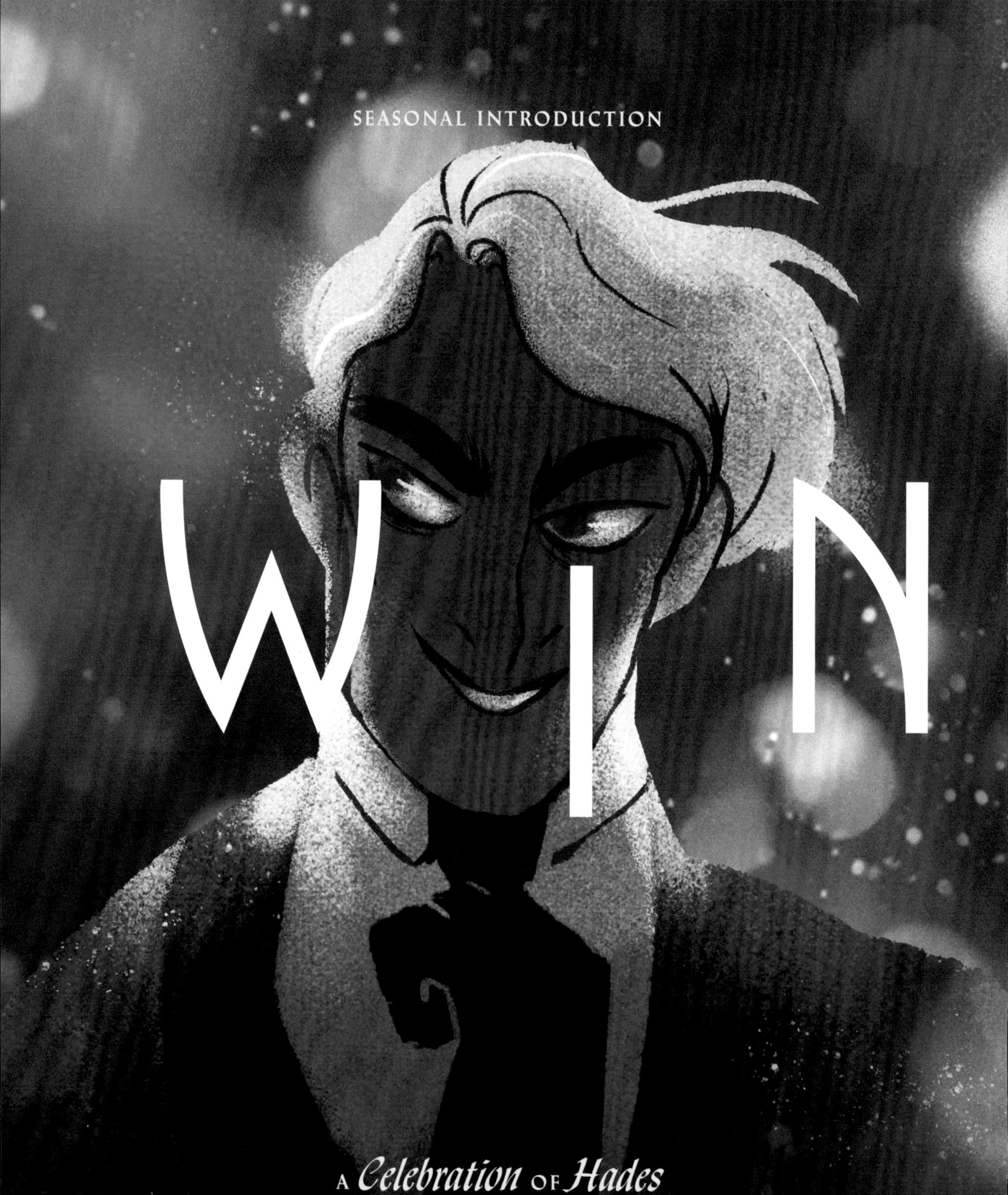

A *Celebration* of *Hades*

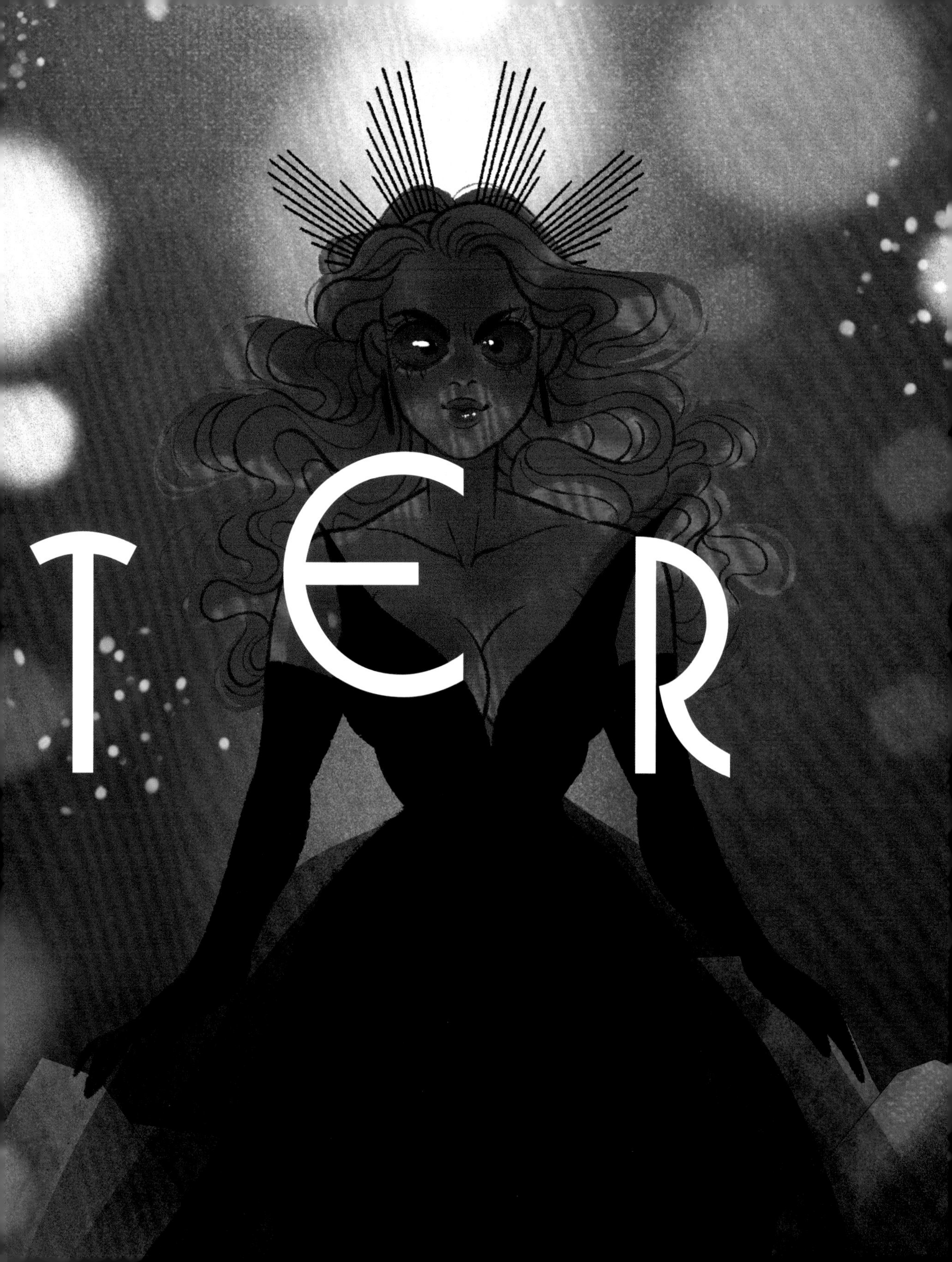
TER

Winter is the season of Hades, and it mirrors his personality at the beginning of *Lore Olympus*. He is chilly and closed off, unyielding and distant. His dark, brooding demeanor is reflected in the landscape of the Underworld, which is the only realm where the sun is not allowed to shine. While some might find this to be a grim place to live, Hades has created his own light—starlight, neon streetlights, and the lights of high-rise buildings—that make the Underworld much more than a dreary and forbidding place.

I know it's not much, but thank you for all your help and kindness
Yours, Rose
Silk
Handkerchief

When Hades first begins his reign in the Underworld, he finds himself contending with older gods and monsters who don't take him seriously. It takes a pact with Erebus to finally allow Hades the right to rule in his realm—a realm that he decides needs to be managed with ruthless efficiency to make order and organization out of the chaos. And to mask his loneliness.

It's not until he meets Persephone that he truly understands the depths of his isolation. He has all the wealth in the world, but no one to spend his money on. He fills the void in his heart with meaningless flings and a toxic relationship with Minthe because he believes that he doesn't deserve to be loved. He initially thinks that the way Minthe treats him—ignoring him, canceling on him, abusing him—is acceptable.

Persephone shows him that he deserves more, that he deserves to feel good and happy and safe. It's a heartbreaking yet happy time for Hades. He gets to share his life and his home—and his *excellent* cooking—with another being. One who loves him. One who cares about him. One who knows the perfect gift for the King of the Underworld is a handkerchief with his beloved Cerberus on it.

In this cold winter, Hades begins to find happiness.

The long nights of this typically harsh season are the happiest evenings for

Hades, because according to mythology, they are when Persephone returns to him. In the original tale, when Persephone ate pomegranate seeds from the Underworld, she was forced to remain there for six months out of the year. She spends half of the year with her mother in the mortal realm, fulfilling her job as the goddess of spring, and the other half of the year in the Underworld, fulfilling her role as Dread Queen. The duality of Persephone's nature is one that mirrors the progression of the roles of women in antiquity: from maiden to formidable matron of their households.

Persephone's role as Dread Queen is noted many times in many different stories. She is mentioned in *The Odyssey* when Odysseus goes to visit his dead mother, she plays a prominent role in the myth of Orpheus and Eurydice, and she is featured in the tale of Eros and Psyche. Once Persephone accepts her role as Dread Queen, Hades is all too happy to give her an equal share of power. They rule together, with her having a true equality that is not seen in other marriages.

Winter is the time of celebration for Hades and Persephone. It is a time of feasting and merriment, of joy after a long parting. It is a time that brightens Hades's drab world and turns it all the colors of spring, allowing the Underworld to feel the heat and magic of the seasons deep under the ground.

Barley Mother's Baklava Porridge

Serves — 4   *Prep time* — 10 minutes   *Cook time* — 1 hour

Is there anything better than barley porridge on a cold winter morning? The sweet, slightly nutty flavor of the barley makes a hearty, wholesome, and filling start to any day. It's a gift from the goddess Demeter, Persephone's mother.

In *Lore Olympus*, Persephone is the heiress to the Barley Mother fortune. Demeter is the CEO and has spent her life feeding the mortal (and immortal) realms while keeping her daughter's existence a secret. It's not the best-kept secret, though, since Persephone's image was co-opted for the company's logo and her face is on every box of Barley Mother cereal, her smile a comforting way to start your day.

This warming winter recipe is another great way to kick off your morning, infused with the flavors of baklava and blessed by the Barley Mother herself.

8 cups (2 L) water

1 cup (200 g) pearl barley or hulled barley, rinsed

2 tablespoons granulated sugar

4 strips lemon peel

¼ teaspoon salt

1½ cups (350 ml) whole milk, plus extra for serving (optional)

1 tablespoon honey, or to taste

2 teaspoons lemon zest

1 teaspoon ground cinnamon

¼ cup (30 g) finely chopped walnuts, plus extra for serving

1. Bring the water to a boil in a large saucepan over high heat. Add the barley, sugar, lemon peel, and salt. Return to a boil, then reduce the heat to medium high and simmer, uncovered, until the barley is tender, 35 to 40 minutes. If using hulled barley instead of pearl barley, you will need to boil for an additional 20 to 25 minutes. Drain any liquid left in the pan and discard the lemon peel.

2. Return the barley to the pan and add the milk, walnuts, honey, lemon zest, and cinnamon. Place over medium-high heat and bring to a boil, then reduce the heat to medium and cook, uncovered, until the mixture thickens, 10 to 15 minutes.

3. Serve the hot barley porridge in bowls with walnuts sprinkled over the top and additional milk, if desired.

Hades's Crispy Hash Browns and Feta Omelet

Serves — 1   *Prep time* — 10 minutes   *Cook time* — 15 minutes

Hades is a wonderful cook. Even though he's a king, he enjoys preparing his own food. And while he doesn't often invite guests to his home, when he does he always treats them with exceptional hospitality—something that was considered an unspoken law in ancient Greece. And whenever Persephone comes over, he makes sure to cater to her dietary preferences, whipping up an out-of-this-world vegetarian-friendly omelet stuffed with rich feta and hash browns.

Omelets are an ideal meal for breakfast (or anytime, really). They are so customizable and allow the ingredients to shine—in this case the melty and tangy feta and the crisp hash browns. Serve with Hermes's Boozy Coffee (page 190) for an indulgent and luxurious start to your weekend.

1 medium yellow potato (see note)
1½ tablespoons extra-virgin olive oil
1 pinch salt
2 eggs, beaten
⅓ cup (50 g) sheep's-milk feta cheese, crumbled
1 pinch dried Greek oregano
1 generous pinch Aleppo pepper flakes (optional)
salt and pepper, to taste

COOK'S NOTE: *You can save time by using frozen shredded hash browns instead! No need to thaw before adding to the pan.*

1. Peel the potato and grate on the large holes of a box grater. Place the grated potato in a colander and rinse well with cold water to remove any excess starch. Place the rinsed potato in the center of a clean tea towel or piece of cheesecloth; gather the cloth and squeeze out as much liquid as possible. Measure a heaping ½ cup (60 g) of shredded potato.

2. Heat the olive oil in an 8-inch (20 cm) nonstick skillet over medium-high heat until hot and shimmery. Add the shredded potato and spread evenly in a thin layer, covering the entire bottom of the skillet. Sprinkle with the salt, reduce the heat to medium, and cook, stirring just once halfway through, until the bottom is dark golden brown and crispy, 7 to 9 minutes.

3. Pour in the beaten egg and tilt the pan in a circular motion to evenly cover the hash browns with egg, but do not stir—you want to leave the hash browns intact on the bottom of the pan. Crumble in the feta and season with the oregano, Aleppo pepper (if using), and salt and pepper. Cover with a lid and cook until the egg is fully set, about 5 minutes.

4. Carefully fold the omelet in half. Remove from the pan and serve immediately.

Xenia
Xenia was the ancient Greek concept of guest rites. It meant that once you welcomed a guest into your home, it was your responsibility to feed them, shelter them, and protect them until they left. Frequently the gods would pretend to be mortals to test how well they were adhering to xenia. This law was taken very seriously, and those who transgressed and treated guests cruelly were punished by the gods— and particularly by Zeus, who was the god who protected strangers.

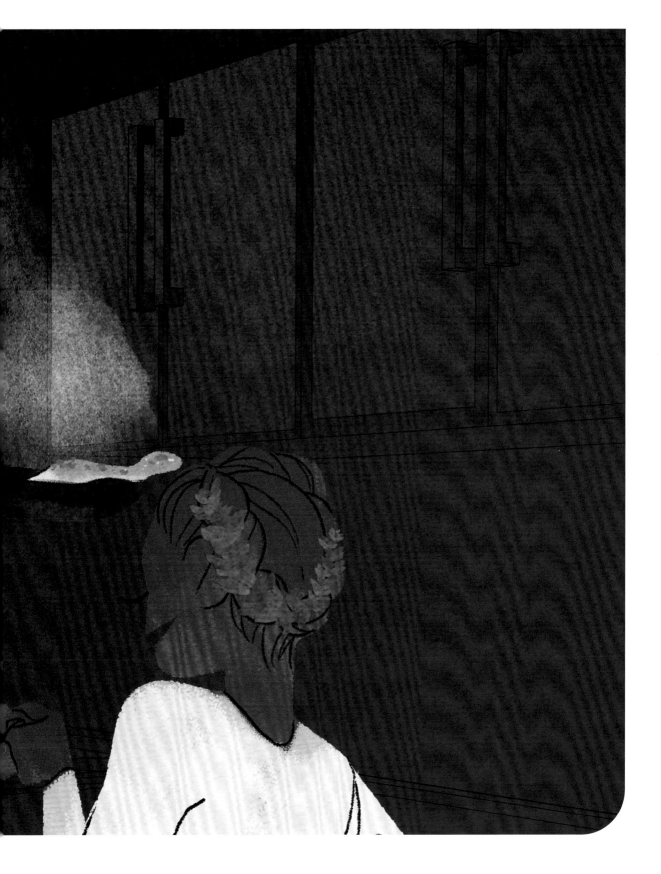

Daphne's Salted Honey Tahini Toast

Yield — 1 cup spread (6 to 8 servings)   *Prep time* — 5 minutes

This salted honey tahini toast is avocado toast's sweet cousin. Tahini is a paste made from sesame seeds and used in lots of Greek dishes, or served on its own as a dip. It is packed with good fats, vitamins, and protein. So, naturally, it's one of Daphne's go-to meals.

Daphne is Olympus's favorite fitness influencer, and she loves to dress up this dish by adding cinnamon, banana, cacao nibs, or sesame seeds to make it an aesthetically pleasing (and simply delicious) dish. Perfect for a meal or a snack—and, of course, for sharing on your socials.

FOR THE SALTED HONEY TAHINI

⅔ cup (170 g) tahini

⅓ cup (110 g) honey, or more to taste

1 teaspoon ground cinnamon

½ teaspoon fleur de sel or coarse sea salt

FOR THE TOAST

thickly sliced sourdough bread

1 pinch fleur de sel or coarse sea salt (optional)

TOPPINGS

½ banana, sliced

2 teaspoons cacao nibs

1 pinch ground cinnamon

1. Make the salted honey tahini: Place the tahini, honey, cinnamon, and fleur de sel or coarse sea salt in a small bowl. Stir well until fully combined.

2. Make the toast: Toast a thick slice of sourdough bread. Spread with some of the tahini mixture. Sprinkle with the fleur de sel, if desired.

3. Top the toast with the banana slices and cacao nibs, then dust with the cinnamon.

TIP: *No need to refrigerate any leftover tahini mixture; just keep it in a jar or other airtight container in a cool, dark place.*

Spiced Tomato-Braised Beef

Serves — 4   *Prep time* — 25 minutes   *Cook time* — 2½ hours

The Furies, or the Kindly Ones, love the taste of blood in the water. They take their job as Hades's enforcers very, *very* seriously, as there is nothing they love more than to mete out justice.

If you find yourself at the mercy of the Kindly Ones, we recommend sharing this riff on a lesser-known Greek dish called kapamas, which has Turkish roots. If there is anything that might get the Furies to stop their mission for a moment, it's this delicious combination of spiced tomato and beef filled with a riot of wintry flavors. Serve with a side of rice, mashed potatoes, or olive-oil-fried potatoes to sate your appetite—and to appease the Furies.

2 lb (900 g) boneless beef chuck
    or tri-tip roast
salt and pepper, to taste
2 tablespoons all-purpose flour
3 tablespoons extra-virgin olive oil
1 small onion, grated
½ cup (120 ml) white wine
3 bay leaves
6 allspice berries
1 teaspoon ground cinnamon
1 teaspoon ground cumin
¼ teaspoon ground cloves
2 cups strained tomatoes (passata)
    or crushed tomatoes
    (about 18 oz / 500 g)
1 teaspoon granulated sugar
    (optional)
2 tablespoons tomato paste
    (optional)

1. If your roast is one large piece, cut it in half against the grain of the meat to make two smaller pieces, which will be easier to work with. Pat dry with paper towels if needed, then season liberally with salt and pepper on all sides. Dust all sides with the flour, shaking off any excess.

2. Heat the olive oil in a medium-sized heavy saucepan or Dutch oven over medium-high heat. Once the oil is hot and shimmering, add the beef and brown on all sides. Remove from the pan and set aside.

3. Reduce the heat to medium. Add the onion and cook until softened, 1 to 2 minutes. Pour in the wine and stir, scraping up any browned bits on the bottom.

4. Add the beef and any accumulated juices back to the pan along with all the spices and the strained tomatoes. Add the sugar, if desired. Pour in enough water to just barely cover the beef, about ½ cup (120 ml) or as needed.

TIP: *It's optional, but the sugar is recommended when using canned tomato products. It balances the acidity and brings out the flavors of the spices.*

The Furies

In Greek mythology, the Furies were feared by everyone. They were tasked with punishing wicked mortals who committed serious crimes, like murder. The Furies were terrifying and would drive their victims to madness. But they were also seen as avenging angels. Throughout antiquity, curse tablets have been found begging for the Furies to appear and grant justice to the wronged and retribution to the wrongful.

5. Cover the pan with a lid and reduce the heat to low. Cook gently until the beef pulls apart easily with a fork, about 2 hours.

6. When the beef is ready, remove the meat to a bowl, increase the heat to medium high, and let the sauce simmer until reduced and thickened. The sauce should not be soupy or watery, but closer to a thick pasta sauce. Add the tomato paste to help thicken the sauce, if desired.

7. When the sauce has thickened, season with salt and pepper. Place the beef back in the pan, warm through, and serve.

Avgolemono

Serves — 4   *Prep time* — 5 minutes   *Cook time* — 30 minutes

Feeling poorly? Under the weather? Caught a dreaded winter cold? While Asclepius, the god of medicine and healing, would probably try to hand you a bunch of leeks as a curative, Hestia would set you up with a bowl of this delicious soup instead.

Avgolemono is sunshine in soup form, and while it is a more recent addition to the Greek diet—invented around 1000 C.E.—it's become a staple of home cooking, and therefore a favorite of the goddess of home and hearth.

8 cups (1 L) chicken stock or bone broth

½ cup (100 g) medium-grain rice, such as Calrose

1 large carrot, finely diced (optional)

1 cup (135 g) shredded cooked chicken (optional)

3 eggs

½ cup (120 ml) freshly squeezed lemon juice, or to taste

salt, to taste

1. Combine the chicken stock, rice, and carrot (if desired) in a large saucepan over medium-high heat. Bring to a boil, then reduce the heat and simmer, partially covered, until the rice is tender, 15 to 20 minutes. Stir in the shredded chicken (if desired) and warm through. Reduce the heat to low.

2. Beat the eggs and lemon juice in a medium bowl with a whisk. Note that you can increase or decrease the amount of lemon juice to taste. If you're a big lemon fan, try increasing it to ⅔ cup (150 ml).

3. Take a ladle of broth from the pan and slowly pour into the egg mixture while whisking constantly. Repeat with 3 to 4 more ladlefuls of broth. Now reverse the process and slowly pour the tempered egg mixture into the rest of the soup in the saucepan while stirring.

4. Increase the heat to medium. Continue to cook and stir until you start to see the first bubbles appear on the surface. Immediately remove from the heat; do not let the soup simmer or boil.

5. Taste and add salt as desired, then serve.

Goddess of the Hearth

While Hestia is the goddess of the home and hearth, she is not always included among the Olympians, as it is sometimes said that she gave up her spot to Dionysus. Her Roman counterpart, Vesta, was so revered as a goddess of the hearth that her priestesses, the Vestal Virgins, kept a sacred flame in her temple that they had to keep constantly burning—on penalty of death.

Prasopita

Serves — 4 to 6   *Prep time* — 25 minutes   *Cook time* — 1 hour

Since ancient times leeks have been valued for both their culinary properties and their healing powers—hence why they are associated with Asclepius, the god of medicine, and Hippocrates, the "father of medicine," who allegedly prescribed leeks for nosebleeds. Leeks were a sign of triumph and victory as well, and were given to athletes when they won a competition. Leeks were ubiquitous throughout ancient Greece as a result.

Feta and leek pie, or prasopita, is the cousin of spanakopita. This crispy, flaky pie is filled with the mildly sweet flavor of leeks and rich feta. It's a delicious, on-the-go dish—exactly the type of thing Asclepius would pack in his medical bag for a meal between house calls.

3 large leeks (about 2 lb / 900 g)

5 to 6 tablespoons extra-virgin olive oil, divided, plus more for greasing

½ teaspoon salt, or more to taste

1 cup (30 g) chopped fresh dill

7 oz (200 g) sheep's-milk feta cheese, crumbled

1 egg, beaten

pepper, to taste

6 to 7 sheets phyllo pastry, thawed if frozen

1½ tablespoons semolina flour

1. Trim the tops and bottoms of the leeks, then cut the white and light green parts into ¼-inch (6 mm) slices. Place in a colander and rinse well to wash away any dirt and sand.

2. Heat 2 tablespoons olive oil in a large frying pan over medium heat. Add the leeks and salt. Cook, stirring occasionally, until the leeks are softened and no liquid remains in the pan, 10 to 15 minutes. Remove from the heat and allow to cool slightly.

3. Preheat the oven to 350 degrees F (180 degrees C). Lightly grease a 9-inch (23 cm) round pan with olive oil.

4. Stir the dill, feta, egg, and pepper into the leek mixture until well combined.

5. Lay out 1 phyllo sheet and lightly brush with olive oil. Transfer to the prepared pan, then repeat with an additional 3 or 4 phyllo sheets.

6. Sprinkle the top phyllo sheet with the semolina flour to prevent a soggy bottom. Spoon the leek mixture evenly over the phyllo base; it shouldn't be more than about a thumb's width thick.

CONTINUED

Multipurpose Leeks

The ancient Egyptians used leeks as something to swear by because they were so venerated. In Rome, Emperor Nero used to eat leeks before he threw his imperial concerts, where he sang for his guests (who were more like captives, as Nero refused to let them leave). And the ancient Goths believed that the only protection from vampires was . . . leeks. If they found themselves without a leek plant, they would carve the symbol of a leek onto a talisman. In short, leeks have had a storied history both inside and outside the kitchen.

7. Fold over the overhanging phyllo sheets. Top with an additional 2 phyllo sheets, brushing each with olive oil and scrunching up the sides around the edge of the pan. Score the top layers into 4 to 6 slices.

8. Bake in the preheated oven until the phyllo is crisp and a deep golden color, 45 to 50 minutes. Remove and let cool slightly before slicing and serving. You can serve this warm or at room temperature.

Coconut Semolina Syrup Cake

Serves — 6 to 9   *Prep time* — 25 minutes   *Cook time* — 20 minutes   *Extra time* — 2 hours, resting

Greek cakes are irresistible, as they're moist, rich, and impossibly light. It's because the cakes are made with love and blessed by Eros himself (well, that might be a stretch; it's probably the olive oil and simple syrup).

Coconut semolina syrup cake is a sponge cake that soaks up the lemony simple syrup it is bathed in, infusing it with flavor. At first you will think the syrup is too much, that it will spoil the cake, but it won't. It's a slow burn—much like the relationship between Eros and Ampelus.

It takes the love god a *very* long time to realize that Ampelus is actually his beloved Psyche, who had been disguised as a nymph by his mother, Aphrodite. But when Eros finally sees Psyche, he is overwhelmed with love for her. Prepare to feel the same level of adoration when you take your first bite of this cake.

FOR THE SYRUP

1¾ cups (400 ml) water
1 cup (200 g) granulated sugar
4 strips lemon peel

FOR THE CAKE

½ cup (110 g) unsalted butter, melted, plus more for greasing the pan
⅓ cup (65 g) granulated sugar
¼ cup (60 ml) whole milk
2 eggs
zest of 1 lemon
1 teaspoon vanilla extract
½ cup (85 g) semolina flour
½ cup (65g) all-purpose flour
½ cup (35 g) finely shredded unsweetened coconut
2 teaspoons baking powder

1. Make the syrup: In a small saucepan, combine the water, sugar, and lemon peel and place over medium heat. Bring to a boil and cook until the sugar is fully dissolved, 1 to 2 minutes. Remove from the heat and let cool completely.

2. Make the cake: Preheat the oven to 350 degrees F (180 degrees C). Grease a 9-inch (23 cm) square cake pan.

3. Stir together the melted butter, sugar, milk, eggs, lemon zest, and vanilla in a large mixing bowl. In a small bowl, combine the semolina flour, all-purpose flour, coconut, and baking powder. Pour the semolina mixture into the butter mixture and fold together until just combined. (The batter will be very thick!) Spoon into the prepared pan and level out to the sides.

4. Bake in the preheated oven until a tester inserted in the center of the cake comes out clean, about 20 minutes.

5. Remove the cake from the oven and immediately pour the cooled syrup over the cake, ladling it bit by bit and letting the syrup gradually soak into the cake. Let the cake rest until the syrup has soaked in fully, about 2 hours.

Pistachio Cherry Icebox Cookies

Yield — 30 cookies *Prep time* — 30 minutes *Cook time* — 15 minutes
Extra time — 30 minutes (if freezing) to 2 hours (if chilling)

Step aside, snickerdoodles. Pistachio, cherry, and dark chocolate cookies are here to take your holiday cookie swap to the next level.

While the ancient Greeks didn't celebrate Christmas, they did have their own winter holidays, which called for feasting, exchanging presents, and drinking *far too much.*

Food in *Lore Olympus* is prepared and shared as a way to express love and comfort. Persephone bakes, Hades cooks (and orders so much takeout!), Eros makes a mean family breakfast, Hestia is the original domestic goddess (literally), and even Artemis has been known to bake on occasion.

These cookies are little homemade parcels of pure joy. Rich dark chocolate, savory pistachios, and bright cherries make these festive-looking treats a perfect expression of love for friends and family during the holidays.

1½ cups (190 g) all-purpose flour

⅔ cup (80 g) powdered sugar

¼ teaspoon salt

⅔ cup (150 g) cold unsalted butter, cubed

2 egg yolks

½ cup (60 g) pistachios, chopped

½ cup (80 g) dried cherries, chopped

4 oz (110 g) dark chocolate, roughly chopped

⅓ cup (40 g) pistachios, finely chopped, for topping

1. Combine the flour, powdered sugar, and salt in a food processor. Add the cubed butter and process in short bursts until the mixture resembles sand. Add the egg yolks and process until the dough comes away from the sides of the bowl and forms a ball. Turn the dough out onto a work surface and gently knead in the chopped pistachios and cherries until evenly distributed throughout the dough.

2. Roll the dough into a log, approximately 1½ inches (4 cm) in diameter and 12 inches (30 cm) long. Wrap in waxed paper or plastic wrap and freeze or chill until firm, 30 to 45 minutes in the freezer or 2 hours in the fridge.

3. Preheat the oven to 325 degrees F (165 degrees C). Line two baking sheets with parchment paper.

4. Unwrap the dough and use a sharp serrated knife to slice it into ¼-inch (6 mm) rounds. Place the rounds on the prepared baking sheets.

CONTINUED

Winter Festivals

In ancient Greece, the winter months of December and January were sacred to Poseidon. However, there was also a festival in January called Haloa, held in honor of Demeter. Haloa marked the end of the sowing season; its name came from the word for "threshing floor." Haloa was a women-only affair, and husbands had to pay for their wives' expenses to attend the festival. This festival was a rowdy, raucous time, filled with cakes shaped like genitalia to invoke fertility, lots of drinking, and plenty of celebration.

5. Bake in the preheated oven until the shortbread is just turning golden around the edges, 15 to 20 minutes. Set aside to cool.

6. Meanwhile, place the chopped chocolate in a glass mixing bowl. Microwave on high power for 30 seconds; remove and stir, then repeat. After the second 30-second interval, microwave just until there are a few chunks of chocolate left, 15 to 30 seconds. Stir until completely smooth.

7. Once the shortbread is cool, set up an assembly line: shortbread, melted chocolate, finely chopped pistachios, and a baking sheet covered with waxed paper or parchment paper. Dip the top half of each shortbread in chocolate, sprinkle with pistachios, and lay on the prepared baking sheet to set. Leave the cookies undisturbed until the chocolate has completely set. If you have space, you can place them in the fridge or freezer to speed up the process.

TIP: *Store the shortbread in an airtight container in layers, separated by sheets of waxed paper or parchment paper.*

Hermes's Boozy Coffee

Serves — 1   *Prep time* — **10 minutes**

Hermes is always on the move. He is constantly working, be it at his main job as messenger of the gods or at his side hustle ferrying souls from the mortal realm to the Underworld. It's almost impossible to catch him sitting (or standing) still. Unless Persephone is cooking; he always makes time for her homemade meals.

As a god on the go, Hermes is a big fan of coffee. He especially loves a decadent booze-filled coffee (with extra whipped cream!).

This coffee spiked with Metaxa is the perfect drink for a busy god or a mortal enjoying a post-dinner aperitif. Rich with notes of brandy, vanilla, and nutmeg—and topped with Hermes's required whipped cream—this is an indulgent treat for those long winter nights.

3 tablespoons heavy whipping cream, chilled

1 teaspoon powdered sugar

⅛ teaspoon vanilla bean paste or vanilla extract

2 teaspoons demerara sugar, or to taste

⅔ cup (150 ml) strong brewed coffee

1½ fl oz (45 ml) Metaxa

freshly grated nutmeg, for serving

1. Combine the cream, powdered sugar, and vanilla in a measuring cup or large glass. Whisk vigorously with a small whisk or milk frother until soft peaks form.

2. Place the sugar in a coffee mug and top with the coffee. Stir to dissolve the sugar. Add the Metaxa, then top with the vanilla cream and a light dusting of freshly grated nutmeg. Enjoy immediately.

Hermes in Mythology
Hermes was one of the youngest Olympians. He was also the trickster of Greek mythology. He loved to steal things: Apollo's cattle (when he was only a day old), Poseidon's trident, Aphrodite's girdle, and Artemis's arrows. Beloved by humans and immortals alike, he was the god of many things, including merchants, thieves, shepherds, boundaries, travelers, and orators, to name just a few.

Warming Winter Ambrosia

Serves — 1   *Prep time* — 5 minutes   *Cook time* — 5 minutes

Winter is the season of cold, and it's a time of sorrow for Demeter. She spends four months of the year mourning her daughter's return to the Underworld, and her grief means that nothing grows, the trees and plants lie dormant, and the weather turns bleak.

So, naturally, it's also the season when Demeter perfects her home-brewed ambrosia.

Ambrosia was said to be the food of the gods. In some myths, it granted immortality to whoever consumed it. It was not a drink for mortals—and those humans who tried to steal it, like Tantalus, were severely punished. Luckily, the *Lore Olympus* Winter Warming Ambrosia won't bring the wrath of the gods down upon you, but this fresh take on a classic Old Fashioned will give you a taste of the divine.

FOR THE HONEY SYRUP
½ cup (180 g) honey
½ cup (120 ml) water

FOR THE COCKTAIL
2 fl oz (60 ml) bourbon
2 teaspoons honey syrup
3 dashes orange bitters
1 strip orange peel, to garnish

1. Make the honey syrup: Combine the honey and water in a small saucepan over medium heat. Bring to a boil, then reduce the heat and simmer just until the honey is completely dissolved and the mixture is homogeneous. Remove from the heat and let cool.

2. Make the cocktail: Fill a cocktail mixing glass with ice. Add the bourbon, honey syrup, and bitters. Stir well. Strain into a rocks glass over ice.

3. Twist the orange peel over the top of the cocktail and then slide it around the rim of the glass. Place the orange twist in the glass and enjoy!

YOUR
PRESENCE
IS REQUESTED

Winter WEDDING *Feast*

Pomegranate, Walnut, and Bulgur Salad pg 201

Hebe's
Pomegranate Spritz
pg 205

Hades's
Chocolate
Lava Cakes
pg 206

Orange Roast
Chicken
and Potatoes
pg 198

Goat Cheese and
Sun-Dried
Tomato Puff
Pastry Star
pg 202

Modeled after Hades and Persephone's wedding reception, this seasonal feast brings together a riot of flavors and a lot of love.

Winter is traditionally a time of scarcity after a period of abundance, but most cultures have some form of midwinter party to celebrate making it through the leaner months, and to revel in the return of the sun. This winter wedding–themed feast focuses on utilizing the comforting tastes of cinnamon, chocolate, orange, pomegranate, and honey—flavors that make us feel warm and safe. Much like how it would feel to dance with a certain King of the Underworld.

But while we can't promise you a spin in Hades's arms—*sigh*—we can deliver on a menu that will make your guests feel like they are at a feast fit for the gods. One that will be talked about throughout the ages, sung about by the muses for all eternity, and hopefully not gossiped about for too long in Olympian Court.

Go easy on the pomegranate spritz.

Orange Roast Chicken and Potatoes

Serves — 6   *Prep time* — 20 minutes   *Cook time* — 1½ to 2 hours

The Fates control the destiny of all mortal and immortal beings. In Greek mythology, the Fates each served a particular purpose. Clotho, Lachesis, and Atropos worked together to spin, measure, and cut the threads of life for all beings. While they have a small part in the *Lore Olympus* story, it is an important one: The Fates manage the library of destiny, where they catalogue the comings and goings of all lives in the world, keeping everything organized on videotape. They are the ones who show Hades the truth of his first meeting with Persephone, helping to draw the pair closer together.

We're also fairly certain there must be a tape in the Fates' library of the first moment you make this dish, because you're destined to fall in love with the zesty orange flavor, succulent chicken, and delightful roast potatoes.

1 cup (240 ml) freshly squeezed orange juice

¼ cup (60 ml) extra-virgin olive oil

¼ cup (60 ml) water

2 tablespoons prepared mustard, such as Dijon or yellow

1½ teaspoons salt

1 teaspoon dried Greek oregano

pepper, to taste

5 large yellow or gold potatoes, peeled (about 2½ lb / 1.2 kg)

1 whole chicken (about 4 lb / 1.8 kg) (see tip)

1. Preheat the oven to 350 degrees F (180 degrees C).

2. In a large mixing bowl, whisk together the orange juice, olive oil, water, mustard, salt, oregano, and pepper. Set aside.

3. Cut each potato in half lengthwise, then slice each half into half-moons about ¼ inch (6 mm) thick. Place the potatoes in the bowl with the orange juice mixture, toss to coat, then scoop into a large roasting pan, letting any excess orange juice mixture drain back into the bowl. Spread the potatoes out evenly in a single layer.

4. Place the chicken in the mixing bowl and coat with the orange juice mixture. Transfer the chicken to the roasting pan, setting it on top of the potatoes. Pour any remaining juice mixture over the chicken.

5. Bake in the preheated oven until the potatoes are tender and the chicken has reached an internal temperature of 165 degrees F (74 degrees C), 1½ to 2 hours.

TIP: *You can follow this recipe using skin-on, bone-in chicken legs or thighs instead. Simply cut the potatoes a little smaller and roast in the oven for approximately 1 hour.*

Pomegranate, Walnut, and Bulgur Salad

Serves — 6   *Prep time* — 10 minutes   *Cook time* — 25 minutes

The artwork in *Lore Olympus*, particularly Persephone's wardrobe, is designed to show a series of contrasts and complements. Especially in the Underworld, Persephone stands out; she is bright and vibrant in a world that is filled with darkness.

Much like Persephone in the Underworld, this winter salad is a light in the darkness. It's guaranteed to brighten up the coldest days with the pop of pomegranate seeds; the fresh taste of mint, lemon, and parsley; and the robust flavors of walnuts and bulgur. Serve as a brilliant side dish, or simply add chicken, feta, or fried halloumi to turn this into a main course.

---

1 cup (180 g) medium bulgur, rinsed

1½ cups (350 ml) water

3 tablespoons plus 1 teaspoon extra-virgin olive oil, divided

1 pinch salt, plus more to taste

pepper, to taste

1 cup (175 g) pomegranate arils (from 1 medium pomegranate)

1 cup (120 g) chopped walnuts

5 green onions, chopped

⅓ cup (10 g) chopped fresh mint

2 tablespoons chopped fresh parsley

juice of 1 lemon

1 tablespoon honey

1. Place the bulgur, water, 1 teaspoon olive oil, and salt in a medium saucepan over high heat. Bring to a boil, then cover and reduce the heat to low. Simmer for 12 to 15 minutes, then remove from heat and let stand until the liquid is absorbed and the bulgur is fluffy, about 10 minutes. Remove the lid and fluff the bulgur with a fork. Set aside to cool.

2. When the bulgur is completely cool, combine with the pomegranate arils, walnuts, green onions, mint, and parsley. Drizzle with 3 tablespoons olive oil, the lemon juice, and honey. Toss to coat, then season with salt and pepper.

Goat Cheese and Sun-Dried Tomato Puff Pastry Star

Serves — 6 to 8   *Prep time* — 20 minutes   *Cook time* — 25 minutes

Beware veiled Titanesses bearing pastries!

This is a lesson that Persephone learns the hard way when her Underworld family barbecue is crashed by Leto, the banished mother of Apollo and Artemis. This Titaness of the heavens brings the brightness of the sun—and a determination to stir up strife in Persephone's love life—into the dark Underworld. However, even a gate-crasher like Leto knows enough to bring a baked good.

This goat cheese, olive, and sun-dried tomato puff pastry star is festive and delicious, and though the star shape makes it a next-level showstopper, it's also surprisingly easy to make. Bring this dish to all of your seasonal get-togethers—or the next time you crash an Underworld bash.

---

4 oz (110 g) soft goat cheese (chèvre)

2 tablespoons grated Pecorino Romano or Kefalotiri cheese

½ cup (75 g) drained chopped sun-dried tomatoes packed in oil

¼ teaspoon dried Greek oregano

pepper, to taste

2 sheets puff pastry, thawed if frozen (approximately 17 oz /500 g)

4 tablespoons chopped Kalamata olives

1 egg, beaten

Asteria

Asteria is Leto's sister and the goddess of fallen stars. She was romantically pursued by Zeus, but unlike Leto, she was not a fan of attention from the king of the gods. Rather than deal with his unwanted advances, she chose to fall from the heavens as a star and turned into the island of Delos.

1. Preheat the oven to 375 degrees F (190 degrees C). Line a baking sheet with parchment paper.

2. Combine the goat cheese, grated cheese, sun-dried tomatoes, oregano, and pepper in a small bowl. Stir well until thoroughly combined.

3. Unroll the first pastry sheet and gently roll with a rolling pin into a square approximately 10 by 10 inches (25 by 25 cm). Trim off the corners to make a circular shape. Transfer to the prepared baking sheet and spread the goat cheese mixture evenly across the whole sheet. Scatter the olives on top.

4. Roll out the second pastry sheet to the same thickness and shape, then transfer it to the baking sheet, laying it on top of the goat cheese mixture.

5. Place a drinking glass in the center of the pastry. Use a sharp knife to cut into quarters around the glass. Cut each quarter into 4 strips. Take the end of a strip and twist two to three times. Repeat with all the strips, then remove the glass. Brush evenly with the beaten egg.

6. Bake in the preheated oven until the pastry is puffy and golden brown, 25 to 30 minutes. Remove and let cool slightly before serving warm.

Hebe's Pomegranate Spritz

Yield — 1½ cups (350 ml) syrup; 1 cocktail *Prep time* — 5 minutes *Cook time* — 25 minutes
Extra time — 30 minutes, cooling

The goddess of youth and daughter of Zeus and Hera, Hebe is also cupbearer to the gods. This gives her an uncanny ability to create the perfect drink, tailored to each god's tastes, even before they order it. It is something that her mother and father shamelessly take advantage of; she is the only one who has successfully mastered Zeus's Golden Appletini (page 157)!

Beyond being the consummate mixologist, Hebe is emotionally intelligent and wise beyond her years. She is always looking out for others, calling them out on their nonsense, and brokering peace between the members of her frequently fractured family.

Hebe's Pomegranate Spritz features prosecco, pomegranate seeds, and spiced pomegranate syrup, making it colorful and festive. It's ideal for winter holidays and certain to become your next favorite cocktail. Praise Hebe.

FOR THE SPICED POMEGRANATE SYRUP

2 cups (475 ml) pomegranate juice
1 cup (200 g) granulated sugar
6 allspice berries
2 whole cloves
2 cinnamon sticks
2-inch (5 cm) piece fresh ginger, peeled and quartered

FOR THE SPICED POMEGRANATE SPRITZ

2 fl oz (60 ml) vodka
1 fl oz (30 ml) Cointreau
1 fl oz (30 ml) spiced pomegranate syrup
4 fl oz (60 ml) prosecco
1 splash sparkling water
½ orange slice, for garnish
pomegranate arils, for garnish

1. Make the spiced pomegranate syrup: Combine the pomegranate juice, sugar, allspice berries, cloves, cinnamon sticks, and ginger in a small saucepan. Place over medium-high heat and bring to a boil, then reduce the heat. Simmer, uncovered, until the liquid has reduced to approximately 1½ cups (350 ml), about 20 minutes.

2. Remove from the heat and set aside. Once the syrup has cooled slightly, strain out the spices and ginger, pour into a jar or measuring cup, and chill in the refrigerator until completely cool. You can store the syrup in the refrigerator for up to 2 weeks.

3. Make the spiced pomegranate spritz: Fill a spritz or red wine glass halfway with ice cubes. Add the vodka, Cointreau, and pomegranate syrup; stir well. Top with the prosecco and sparkling water, then garnish with the orange slice and pomegranate arils.

TIP: *For a zero-proof version, add the pomegranate syrup to a mix of 3 fl oz (90 ml) sparkling water and 3 fl oz (90 ml) sparkling apple juice.*

Hades's Chocolate Lava Cakes

Serves — 4   *Prep time* — 20 minutes   *Cook time* — 10 minutes

In addition to being the god of the Underworld, wealth, and the dead, Hades is also associated with volcanoes. While Hephaestus is more commonly known as the volcano god, volcanoes are intrinsically tied to Hades because he ruled everything that was under the ground. And as volcanoes could be the catalysts for both life (formations of new lands, fertile soil) and death (catastrophic eruptions), they served as a symbol for Hades. One of the most famous entrances to the Underworld is through a volcanic vent near Mount Etna, in Sicily, where Hades was said to be born.

In the *Lore Olympus* universe, Hades has quite the sweet tooth, and these chocolate olive oil lava cakes are a pitch-perfect blend of sinfully dark chocolate and light sponge cake—perfect for the King of the Underworld.

½ cup (120 g) extra-virgin olive oil, plus more for greasing

2 tablespoons all-purpose flour, plus more for dusting

1 cup (170 g) semisweet chocolate chips

3 eggs, at room temperature

⅓ cup (65 g) granulated sugar

2 teaspoons unsweetened cocoa powder

1 pinch salt

1. Preheat the oven to 400 degrees F (200 degrees C). Grease four 6-ounce ramekins and dust with flour, tapping out any excess.

2. Place the olive oil and chocolate chips in a microwave-safe bowl. Microwave on full power for 30 seconds at a time, stirring between intervals. Once the chips are almost all melted, stir well until they melt completely. Set aside.

3. In a large mixing bowl, beat the eggs and sugar with an electric mixer on high speed until pale in color, 4 to 5 minutes. Fold in the chocolate mixture, flour, cocoa powder, and salt. Place the ramekins on a baking sheet and divide the batter between them.

4. Bake in the preheated oven until the edges of the cakes are set but the center is still soft, 9 to 12 minutes. Let sit on the baking sheet for 1 minute, then carefully invert each ramekin on a dessert plate. Serve these cakes on their own, or with the vanilla mascarpone cream from the Red Wine Pomegranate Poached Pears on page 136.

Acknowledgments

FROM GENN McMENEMY

A massive thank-you to the brilliant Rachel Smythe, Sarah Peed, and WEBTOON for trusting me with this project. This has been a dream come true for me. Thanks to my mom and dad, who unfailingly believed in me. Thank you to these goddesses for your endless support—Liv Albert, Jenny Williamson, Angela Marshall, Porsche McGovern, and my agent, Ellen Scordato. Thank you to my family, who have endured me while I spouted random mythology facts at them—Patrick McMenemy and Jennifer Schellenberg, and Gregory McMenemy, Melissa Young, and Elizabeth Young. And big thanks to my husband, Glen, and our dogs, Triss and Jake.

FROM DIANA MOUTSOPOULOS

Foremost, I wish to thank my husband, Raghav, and children, Aris and Athina, for their endless encouragement. My mom and sister, my biggest cheerleaders. My family in Greece, who laid the foundation for my love of Greek cuisine. My Geneva and Delhi family for all of their support. Friends who've always believed in me (you know who you are!). And my editor, Sarah Peed, for her guidance and giving me this amazing opportunity.

FROM RACHEL SMYTHE

Thank you to Genn McMenemy for bringing the project to life with not only her passion for *Lore Olympus* but also her vast knowledge of Greek history and mythology. Diana Moutsopoulos, the heart of this book, thank you for sharing your culture by creating these beautiful recipes and adding to the world of *Lore Olympus* in a truly meaningful way. And thank you, Eva Kolenko, for the absolutely stunning photography that feels faithful to the comic but also completely unique!

Art Assistants:

Kristina Ness	Jaki King	Mary Nowak
Jaki Haboon	Amy Kim	Court Rogers
Yulia Garibova (Hita)	Karen Pavon	Johana R. Ahumada
Lissette Carrera	Chelsie Burns	M. Rawlings

Index

Notes

Notes

About the Authors

RACHEL SMYTHE is the creator of the Eisner Award–winning *Lore Olympus*, published via WEBTOON.

X: @used_bandaid

INSTAGRAM: @usedbandaid

LoreOlympusBooks.com

GENN McMENEMY is the author of *Women of Myth* and the co-host of the *Ancient History Fangirl* podcast. She is an author, freelance marketer, and podcaster.

X: @gennmcmenemy

INSTAGRAM: @gennmcmenemy

DIANA MOUTSOPOULOS is a food writer, recipe developer, Greek cuisine expert, and editorial director at Allrecipes. She has showcased her culinary skills on E! News and is the founder of International Feta Day, a celebration of one of Greece's most iconic ingredients. She lives in Los Angeles with her husband, Raghav, and their two children, Aris and Athina.

INSTAGRAM: @greek_recipes

Published in the United States by Random House Worlds, an imprint of
Random House, a division of Penguin Random House LLC, New York.

RANDOM HOUSE is a registered trademark, and RANDOM HOUSE WORLDS
and colophon are trademarks of Penguin Random House LLC.

Hardback ISBN 978-0-593-79823-2
Ebook ISBN 978-0-593-79824-9

Printed in China

randomhousebooks.com

Editor: Sarah Peed
Production editor: Ted Allen
Art director: Jenny Davis
Designer: Walter Green
Logo design: Cassie Gonzales
Illustrations: Rachel Smythe
Photography and art direction: Eva Kolenko
Prop stylist: Genesis Vallejo
Food stylist: Natalie Drobny
Food stylist assistants: Paige Arnett and Allison Fellion
Production manager: Erin Korenko
Copy editor: Sue Warga
Proofreaders: Melanie Gold,
    Barb Jatkola, Becky Maines, and Tess Rossi
Indexer: Charlee Trantino

9 8 7 6 5 4 3 2 1

First Edition